ECONOMIC ISSUES, PROBLEMS AND PERSPECTIVES

NATIONAL AND MANDATORY FLOOD INSURANCE

ECONOMIC ISSUES, PROBLEMS AND PERSPECTIVES

Additional books in this series can be found on Nova's website under the Series tab.

Additional E-books in this series can be found on Nova's website under the E-books tab.

NATURAL DISASTER RESEARCH, PREDICTION AND MITIGATION

Additional books in this series can be found on Nova's website under the Series tab.

Additional E-books in this series can be found on Nova's website under the E-books tab.

ECONOMIC ISSUES, PROBLEMS AND PERSPECTIVES

NATIONAL AND MANDATORY FLOOD INSURANCE

ANNA M. MUÑOZ
AND
MEGAN O. PHILLIPS
EDITORS

Nova Science Publishers, Inc.
New York

For permission to use material from this book please contact us:
Telephone 631-231-7269; Fax 631-231-8175
Web Site: http://www.novapublishers.com

LIBRARY OF CONGRESS CATALOGING-IN-PUBLICATION DATA

National and mandatory flood insurance / editors, Anna M. Muñoz and Megan O. Phillips.
p. cm. -- (Economic issues, problems and perspectives) (Natural disaster research, prediction and mitigation)
Includes bibliographical references and index.
ISBN 978-1-61209-126-6 (hardcover : alk. paper)
1. Flood insurance--United States. 2. National Flood Insurance Program (U.S.) I. Muñoz, Anna M. II. Phillips, Megan O.
HG9983.3.N368 2011
368.1'22200973--dc22
2010047062

Published by Nova Science Publishers, Inc. † New York

CONTENTS

PREFACE

While most young people have access to emotional and financial support systems throughout their early adult years, older youth in foster care and those who are emancipated from care often face obstacles to developing independent living skills and building supports that ease the transition to adulthood. Older foster youth who return to their parents or guardians may continue to experience poor family dynamics or a lack of emotional and financial supports. This new book provides an overview of the federal foster care system and provisions in federal foster care law that are intended to help prepare youth for adulthood.

Chapter 1- In 1968, the U.S. Congress established the National Flood Insurance Program (NFIP) to address the nation's flood exposure and challenges inherent in financing and managing flood risks in the private sector. Private insurance companies at the time claimed that the flood peril was uninsurable and, therefore, could not be underwritten in the private insurance market. A three-prong floodplain management and insurance program was created to (1) identify areas across the nation most at risk of flooding; (2) minimize the economic impact of flooding events through floodplain management ordinances; and (3) provide flood insurance to individuals and businesses. Major changes were made to the program in 1973, 1994, and 2004.

Chapter 2- The National Flood Insurance Program (NFIP), established in 1968, provides policyholders with insurance coverage for flood damage. The Federal Emergency Management Agency (FEMA) within the Department of Homeland Security is responsible for managing NFIP. Unprecedented losses from the 2005 hurricane season and NFIP's periodic need to borrow from the U.S. Treasury to pay flood insurance claims have raised concerns about the program's long-term financial solvency. Because of these concerns and

NFIP's operational issues, NFIP has been on GAO's high-risk list since March 2006. As of August 2010, NFIP's debt to Treasury stood at $18.8 billion. This testimony discusses (1) NFIP's financial challenges, (2) FEMA's operational and management challenges, and (3) actions needed to address these challenges. In preparing this statement, GAO relied on its past work on NFIP and GAO's ongoing review of FEMA's management of NFIP, particularly data management and contractor oversight issues.

Chapter 3- This chapter examines the amount of flood insurance that must be purchased (and retained) on loans secured by real property located in federally designated special flood hazard areas (SFHAs). It is written in response to three situations: (1) the Federal Emergency Management Agency's remapping efforts that include verifying the status of all levees as providing protection against a 100-year flood, which are currently depicted on Flood Insurance Rate Maps, and widespread concerns among homeowners about new requirements to purchase flood insurance should the levee become decertified; (2) uncertainty as to whether the mandatory amount of flood insurance should be equal to the assessed value of the insured residential structure or the unpaid principal balance (UPB) of the mortgage loan; and (3) concerns that homeowners may be inappropriately asked to purchase an amount of flood insurance that is several times the value of the actual property.

Chapter 4- In the aftermath of Hurricanes Katrina and Rita in 2005, homeowners in Louisiana, Mississippi, and Alabama protested what they view as inappropriate obstacles to the payment of their property_ damage insurance claims. When insurance adjustors and damage experts assessed the properties damaged by the 2005 storms, they were faced with the issue of allocating damages between wind (a covered loss) and flood (an excluded loss). The delays and economic uncertainty that this activity has engendered have raised financial and legal issues for insurers, as well as homeowners and businesses along the Gulf Coast region.

Chapter 5- Questions about the financial status of the National Flood Insurance Program (NFIP) have increased since the 2005 hurricanes, which left the program with an unprecedented $17.4 billion deficit—a debt that resulted in GAO placing NFIP on its high-risk list in March 2006. Among the concerns are the subsidized rates NFIP must provide for about 25 percent of the policies, mostly for older buildings in high-risk flood zones. And although fully risk-based rates are supposed to reflect actual flood risk, concerns have been raised that they do not. This chapter evaluates (1) the Federal Emergency Management Agency's (FEMA) process for setting full-risk rates to determine whether it produces rates that accurately reflect the risk of flooding and (2) the process that FEMA uses to set subsidized rates and their effect on the financial condition of NFIP. To do this work, GAO evaluated the NFIP rate model, examined data from FEMA, surveyed relevant literature, and interviewed other relevant agencies and risk-modeling firms.

In: National and Mandatory Flood Insurance ISBN: 978-1-61209-126-6
Editors: A. Muñoz and M. Phillips

Chapter 1

NATIONAL FLOOD INSURANCE PROGRAM: BACKGROUND, CHALLENGES, AND FINANCIAL STATUS

Rawle O. King

SUMMARY

In 1968, the U.S. Congress established the National Flood Insurance Program (NFIP) to address the nation's flood exposure and challenges inherent in financing and managing flood risks in the private sector. Private insurance companies at the time claimed that the flood peril was uninsurable and, therefore, could not be underwritten in the private insurance market. A three-prong floodplain management and insurance program was created to (1) identify areas across the nation most at risk of flooding; (2) minimize the economic impact of flooding events through floodplain management ordinances; and (3) provide flood insurance to individuals and businesses. Major changes were made to the program in 1973, 1994, and 2004.

The NFIP was self-supporting from 1986 until 2005 as policy premiums and fees covered all expenses and claim payments. In 2005, the NFIP incurred approximately $17 billion in flood claims caused by Hurricanes Katrina, Rita, and Wilma. This amount exceeded the $2.2 billion in annual premiums and the $1.5 billion in borrowing authority from the U.S. Treasury. As a result, Congress passed and the President signed into law legislation to increase NFIP borrowing authority first to $3.5 billion (P.L. 109-65) and then to $18.5 billion (P.L. 109-106) in November 2005, and finally to $20.775 billion (P.L. 109-208) on March 23, 2006. As of March 31, 2010, the outstanding debt and accrued interest cost stood at $18.75 billion. Under current law, the funds borrowed from the U.S. Treasury must be repaid with interest. The program, however, is not in a position to repay the debt.

The 111th Congress has acted to ensure that basic NFIP authorities remain in force while the debate continues on reform proposals. On May 31, 2010, however, FEMA's authority to issue or renew flood insurance policies or to increase coverage on existing policies under the NFIP lapsed for the third time this year. On July 2, 2010, President Barack Obama signed into law H.R. 5569, the National Flood Insurance Program Extension Act, to retroactively reauthorize the program from June 1, 2010, through September 30, 2010 (P.L. 111-196). Although FEMA is now authorized to issue new policies and pay claims, concerns remain about the possibility of yet another lapse in authority after September 30, 2010.

Meanwhile, on May 26, 2010, the House Committee on Financial Services reported H.R. 5114, the Flood Insurance Reform Priorities Act of 2010, to reauthorize the NFIP through FY2015 and to make certain reforms to the program. These reforms include (1) a phase-in of actuarial rates for non-residential properties and non-primary residences; (2) a delay in the effective date for the mandatory purchase of flood insurance for certain areas not previously designated as having a special flood hazard; (3) a five-year phase-in of flood insurance rates for newly mapped areas not previously designated as having special flood hazard; (4) an increase in the annual limitation on premium increases; (5) the establishment of the Office of Flood Insurance Advocate; and (6) commission of several studies on expanding mandatory flood insurance purchase requirements for low-income families, and building codes. A vote on H.R. 5114 is expected in the House of Representatives in mid-July 2010. There is no similar measure in the Senate.

Several other flood insurance-related bills are currently before the 111th Congress: H.R. 1264 would add wind coverage to the NFIP; H.R. 777 would suspend flood map changes until the Administrator of FEMA submits to Congress a community outreach plan.

This chapter provides an analysis of the National Flood Insurance Program (NFIP) and its financial status, summarizes the major challenges facing the program, including issues affecting its long-term financial solvency, presents some alternative approaches for managing and financing the flood losses and describes pending legislation on this issue.

RECENT DEVELOPMENT: FLOOD INSURANCE AUTHORITY LAPSE

The 111th Congress has acted to ensure that basic NFIP authorities remain in force while the debate continues on proposals for comprehensive reform and modernization of the program.[1] On May 31, 2010, however, FEMA's authority to issue or renew flood insurance policies or to increase coverage on existing policies under the NFIP lapsed for the third time this year. On July 2, 2010, President Barack Obama signed into law H.R. 5569, the National Flood Insurance Program Extension Act, to retroactively reauthorize the program from June 1, 2010, through September 30, 2010.[2] Although FEMA is now authorized to issue new policies and pay claims, concerns remain about the possibility of yet another lapse in authority after September 30, 2010.

As background, under the NFIP, lenders are prohibited from making, increasing, extending, or renewing loans secured by improved real property or a mobile home located in a special flood hazard area (SFHA) where federal flood insurance is available unless the building or mobile home is covered by flood insurance.[3] This requirement is satisfied with coverage obtained from the NFIP.

During the recent lapse in FEMA's authority, borrowers were not able to obtain NFIP insurance to close, renew, or increase loans secured by property located in SFHA until the NFIP is reauthorized. To address consumer concerns about having to wait to close on the sale of a property within an SFHA or current policyholders' uncertainty about coverage for flood damages during the lapsed period of NFIP authorization, FEMA issued informal guidance to Write Your Own (WYO) insurance companies and the program's servicing agents.[4]

The Federal Reserve Board (FRB),[5] the Office of the Comptroller of the Currency (OCC), and Fannie Mae issued guidance to national banks, savings associations, and mortgage lenders informing them that they are authorized to make loans during the hiatus that are or will be secured by property located in flood hazard areas—that is, they will not be cited for violating federal flood insurance regulations for not obtaining flood insurance coverage while it is not available through the NFIP.

OCC provided guidance to assist national banks in dealing with the period during which FEMA's authority to issue flood insurance policies under the NFIP lapses.[6] OCC indicated that national banks may continue to make loans without flood insurance during a period when the NFIP is not available.

Lenders must still comply with other parts of the federal flood insurance regulations,[7] such as making flood determinations, issuing accurate notices to borrowers, and prudently managing their portfolio of flood-insured property risks during the lapse period. Also, regulated financial institutions must have a system in place to ensure that flood policies on properties that are subject to mandatory flood insurance coverage are obtained as soon as possible after the NFIP is reauthorized.

A lender has the option to have the borrower complete the flood insurance application, pay the premium, and have the insurance company hold the application for processing pending congressional reauthorization. The lender could also opt to postpone closing the loan until after the NFIP has been reauthorized or have the borrower obtain private flood insurance where available. The private insurance option could be costly.

Fannie Mae provides financing to the mortgage market by buying the loans from lenders. Fannie Mae typically cannot purchase mortgages on properties without adequate flood insurance. However, Fannie Mae announced that it would continue to purchase mortgage loans secured by properties in SFHA, even without an active flood insurance policy, provided that Congress retroactively reauthorizes the program.[8] Fannie Mae requires the borrower to provide evidence of applying for flood insurance, including a copy of the application, check or the final HUD-1 Settlement Statement showing payment of the initial premium. Fannie Mae requires the lender to have a process in place to identify mortgaged properties that do not provide proper evidence of active flood insurance.

Meanwhile, on May 26, 2010, the House Committee on Financial Services reported H.R. 5114, the Flood Insurance Reform Priorities Act of 2010, to reauthorize the NFIP through FY2015 and to make certain reforms to the program. These reforms include (1) a phase-in of actuarial rates for non-residential properties and non-primary residences; (2) a delay in the effective date for the mandatory purchase of flood insurance for certain areas not previously designed as having a special flood hazard; (3) a five-year phase-in of flood insurance rates for newly mapped areas not previously designated as having special flood hazard; (4) an increase in the annual limitation on premium increases; (5) the establishment of the Office of Flood Insurance Advocate; and (6) commission of several studies on expanding mandatory flood insurance purchase requirements for low-income families, and building codes. A vote on H.R. 5114 is expected in the House of Representatives in mid-July 2010.

BACKGROUND

Table 1. Top Fifteen Significant Flood Events Covered by the National FloodInsurance Program (1978-March 31, 2009; $ Nominal)

Rank	Event	Date	Number of Paid Losses	Amount Paid	Average Paid Loss
1	Hurricane Katrina	Aug. 2005	166,682	$16,055,393,803	$96,324
2	Hurricane Ike	Sept. 2008	43,926	2,331,208,210	53,071
3	Hurricane Ivan	Sept. 2004	27,585	1,573,349,939	57,036
4	Tropical Storm Allison	June 2001	30,662	1,103,765,221	35,998
5	Louisiana Flood	May 1995	31,343	585,072,008	18,667
6	Hurricane Isabel	Sept. 2003	19,850	491,504,384	24,761
7	Hurricane Rita	Sept. 2005	9,468	463,278,852	48,931
8	Hurricane Floyd	Sept. 1999	20,439	462,270,253	22,617
9	Hurricane Opal	Oct. 1995	10,343	405,528,543	39,208
10	Hurricane Hugo	Sept. 1989	12,843	376,493,066	29,315
11	Hurricane Wilma	Oct. 2005	9,599	363,036,286	37,820
12	Nor'Easter	Dec. 1992	25,141	346,151,231	13,768
13	Midwest Flood	June 1993	10,472	272,827,070	26,053
14	PA, NJ, NY Floods	June 2006	6,410	226,830,179	35,387
15	Nor'Easter	Apr. 2007	8,628	224,814,700	26,056

Source: Federal Emergency Management Agency, U.S. Department of Homeland Security.

Historically, floods have been among the most costly natural disasters in the United States. Flooding along river banks has been a main public policy concern for years. An additional challenge today is flooding caused by weather-related coastal hazards—hurricanes, storm surges, and tornadoes—that are increasing in frequency and severity, creating an unprecedented threat to U.S. coastlines and Midwestern states where floods that would historically occur once every 20 years are projected to happen every four to six years.[9] This situation has become a concern of policymakers because more than half of the U.S. population now live in coastal watershed counties or floodplain areas and approximately 50% of the nation's gross domestic product ($4.5 trillion in 2000) is generated in those Gulf and Atlantic coastal areas.[10] One estimate from Lloyds of London and Risk Management Solutions (RMS) predicts that flood losses along the Gulf and Atlantic coastlines would increase 80% by 2030 with a one foot rise in the sea level.[11] The corresponding surge in economic losses from coastal hazards arguably demands a national policy response to better manage the costs of existing coastal risks.

Table 1 provides a list of the top fifteen flood events in the United States in terms of NFIP payouts. The devastation from Hurricane Katrina emerged as a pivotal event in the history of federal flood control policy, with wind and flooding estimated to have caused over $200 billion in economic damages (both insured and uninsured) and more than 1,700 deaths. Hurricane Katrina convinced many of a trend increase in the cost of floods and the frequency of major flood disasters.

Governments in the United States have a long history of regulating private economic activity for the purpose of promoting economic recovery and protecting or supporting particular economic groups. For example, economic uncertainty stemming from widespread flooding in the mid-1960s, the need for economic relief and recovery for flood victims, and calls for a reduction in the financial burden on taxpayers led to economic regulation of the nation's floodplains and insurance markets. The government became a regulator of certain economic activity in flood-prone areas to reduce the physical and economic risks associated with flood hazards. In the absence of a sufficient supply of insurance to meet societal demand, the government took action to safeguard the economic interests of consumers, businesses, communities, and taxpayers.

Economic regulation was accomplished in two ways. First, the government acted to limit the discretion of individuals and companies engaged in economic activity in flood prone areas. Depending on whether a building is located in a government-designated SFHA, flood insurance may be required as a condition of obtaining a federally secured mortgage loan. Homeowners typically discover they need flood insurance during the home-buying process that includes a disclosure of where the property is located relative to the SFHA that is mapped on a flood insurance rate map (FIRM).

Second, economic regulation was accomplished through "managerial regulation," with the government providing subsidized flood insurance for individuals and businesses in communities that undertook specific steps to regulate the floodplain through land use zoning ordinances and building standards.[12]

In the wake of Hurricanes Katrina, Rita, and Wilma in 2005, Hurricane Ike and the Midwest floods of 2008, and the New England region floods in 2010, Members of Congress may wish to examine the viability of the NFIP's structure, function and financial solvency. Some also question whether the government should continue to underwrite insurance in support of coastal development and rebuilding in flood-prone areas. Meanwhile, federal expenditures for federal relief payments and insurance claims in coastal communities and along riverbanks continue to be a major challenge for the NFIP.

ECONOMIC REGULATION AND RECOVERY FROM FLOOD HAZARDS

Congress has a responsibility through the "general welfare" and "interstate commerce" clauses of the U.S. Constitution to promote national economic growth. One factor affecting the nation's economic well-being is the proper functioning of markets for natural disaster risk: do economic markets provide a sufficient amount of insurance against flood hazards? Further, to the extent that flood insurance exists, are the insuring firms sufficiently capitalized so that widespread insolvencies would not occur? These were just a few of the key questions the nation faced in the 1960s, as hurricanes caused increased havoc along the U.S. Gulf and Atlantic coasts.

There were four very broad underlying causes for economic regulation—government intervention—in the market for flood insurance in the 1960s. *First*, people insisted that social and ethical values as well as economic values should be reflected in the operation of the economy. Persons suffering economic distress or dislocation from flood hazards sought and received governmental aid in dealing with their problem. The aid was in the form of disaster relief assistance, subsidized flood insurance, and government spending on flood risk identification and mapping.

Second, government action was viewed as being necessary to bring about more efficient coordination and utilization of resources. Economic regulatory programs were thought to be needed to prescribe certain land use zoning ordinances and building code standards to govern economic or business behavior to reduce the physical and economic risks associated with coastal hazards.

Third, as the nation experienced widespread flooding in the 1960s, people became interested in their personal security and, thus, in shifting some or all of the risk of economic life from themselves to government. In response, policymakers changed the way economic risk of flooding was defined and the means of achieving security for the individual. Economic hazards, whether man-made or natural, were initially considered inevitable or "acts of God" but came to be viewed as public problems that required government action to protect individuals, businesses, communities, and taxpayers. Government assistance in the form of subsidized insurance premiums was viewed as a solution to reduce the future costs and risks of investing in flood-prone areas.

Fourth, sole reliance on insurance markets for flood risks was not an option. This situation provided a rationale for possible government intervention in the economy to ensure that the costs and benefits of living in flood-prone areas were not ignored. Individuals and insurers at risk of flooding, however, have in the past lacked the information necessary for the market system to operate effectively. Insurers did not always have flood hazard maps, as they do now, and thus had no reliable, consistent, and cost-effective way to identify and assess flood risk. Homeowners did not and sometimes still do not, have the information needed to make rational economic decisions about real estate investments. All this resulted in a misallocation of resources which required and still requires government intervention to protect the public interest.

EVOLUTION OF THE NATIONAL FLOOD INSURANCE PROGRAM

Flood hazards in the United States, whether from hurricanes and the impact of storm surge on property or inland flooding on rivers, lakes and streams, was largely deemed commercially uninsurable. The standard multiperil homeowners insurance did not provide coverage against flood hazards. Floods were perceived to be uninsurable for three reasons: (1) adverse selection meant that only individuals in flood-prone areas would purchase coverage; (2) risk-based premiums were too costly for the average household; and (3) insurers could not generate sufficient premiums to insure against a catastrophic flood event. Government mapping of areas prone to flooding, subsidized flood insurance, and floodplain management regulations were key to the program's structure and function. These concerns about flood insurance market failure led to the passage of the National Flood Insurance Act of 1968.

Traditional insurance principles indicated that private insurers would not be able to gather a large enough pool of independent risks to allow the actuarial technique of "law of large numbers" to reduce the risk. Most property owners in floodplains usually face the same flood hazard and their risks tend to be highly correlated—not independent. Correlated risks means the insurer must charge higher premiums to reflect a larger risk load or administrative cost that accounts for the uncertainty faced by the insurer in predicting future losses of the pool. In other words, the premium level that private insurers needed to adequately underwrite flood hazards would be so high that few would be willing to purchase coverage.

The NFIP was a public policy response to the flood peril and escalating costs of taxpayer-funded disaster relief for flood victims. Federally backed flood insurance was made available to home and business owners in communities that voluntarily agreed to adopt and enforce floodplain management ordinances designed to reduce flood-related property losses. The creation of the NFIP marked a significant shift in U.S. flood control policy away from a "levee-only" flood reduction approach towards a risk identification, risk financing and floodplain management approach that was intended to foster individual responsibility and build local self-sufficiency in terms of land-use zoning ordinances and construction standards.

Federal flood insurance was considered to be an economically efficient way to indemnify flood victims and to have individuals internalize some of the risk of locating property in the floodplains.[13] The federal government would utilize its capacity to spread losses over time with the NFIP's ability to borrow money from the U.S. Treasury to offset program deficits. A federal government insurance program, it was thought, could also link the availability of flood insurance to land use regulation and building codes that would, in theory, reduce long-term flood risk.

Today, under the NFIP, the federal government is required to take certain actions to:

- identify and map areas across the country that are at high risk of flooding;
- indemnify individuals and businesses against flood losses by making floodinsurance widely available at actuarially sound rates or with legally mandatedpremium subsidies; and
- reduce future flood losses through floodplain management regulations andactions.[14]

The NFIP has undergone major changes largely in response to significant flood events over the years. For example, the program was created after Hurricane Betsy devastated the Gulf Coast in 1965. After Hurricane Agnes in 1972, recognizing the low market penetration of flood insurance, Congress enacted the Flood Disaster Protection Act of 1973[15] to establish a mandatory flood insurance purchase requirement for structures located in identified SFHA. After the 1973 Act, federally regulated lenders were obligated to require flood insurance on any loan secured by improved real estate in a FEMA-designated SFHA in a participating community.

After the 1993 Midwest floods, it became apparent to Congress that homeowners were still not adequately complying with the mandatory insurance purchase requirement. The Midwest flood of 1993 provided the impetus for strengthening lender compliance through the mandatory purchase provisions in the 1994 National Flood Insurance Reform Act.[16] Recognition of the impact of properties prone to repetitive flooding on the financial condition of the program led to the passage of the Flood Insurance Reform Act of 2004[17] which established a pilot program for the mitigation of severe repetitive—loss properties (SRLPs) and the funding of mitigation activities for individual SRLPs.

Although the NFIP faces many challenges, and there is widespread agreement that the program needs to be reformed, the evidence continues to suggest broad support for the basic principle of using an insurance pooling mechanism for those who have chosen to live in high-risk areas. Some of the policy questions for the 111th Congress include the following: Is the NFIP currently encouraging unwise construction in floodplains? Are taxpayers subsidizing unwise construction as a result of inaccurate maps? If the program does encourage unwise construction or rebuilding in high-risk areas without proper first-floor elevation, what steps should policymakers take to keep the promises of safer construction made to taxpayers at the inception of the program? If premiums are inadequate to finance programs, is Treasury debt the only answer?

Lessons from Katrina and the 2008 Midwest Floods

The 2008 Atlantic hurricane season was among the costliest on record for flood losses and resulted in a large infusion of taxpayers' money to cover uninsured disaster losses. Hurricane Ike alone caused about $2.3 billion in NFIP claims along the coastal areas of Texas and Louisiana and further inland, including many areas not typically subject to tropical rain events. In addition to flooding from Hurricane Ike there was extensive 500-year flood damage in the Midwest that was not anticipated by current out-of-date methodologies. According to FEMA, more than 11 million people in nine Midwestern states were affected by the 2008 Midwest floods as major rivers in Illinois, Indiana, Iowa, Kansas, Michigan, Minnesota, Missouri, Nebraska, and Wisconsin overflowed their banks and levees. Especially hard hit states were Iowa, Indiana, and Illinois, where the river levels surpassed levels reached in the Great Flood of 1993.

Although the 2008 Midwest floods caused dozens of levees to be breached, destroying thousands of homes and businesses, and inundating thousands of acres of agricultural cropland, the flooding did not rank among the NFIP's top 15 most costly events. Payments under the NFIP were relatively low because of low flood insurance purchases in the affected areas. Similarly, although the 1993 Midwest flood was the most devastating flooding in the region's history, it ranks 13th among the leading NFIP flood events with $273 million in NFIP claims.

In 2005, the devastating flooding caused by Hurricanes Katrina and Rita resulted in approximately $200 billion in economic losses, of which $21.9 billion will likely be covered under the NFIP. The massive flood losses from Hurricanes Katrina and Rita financially overwhelmed the NFIP. It also focused public attention on (1) the economics of government risk-bearing through federal flood insurance when private insurers do not offer affordable coverage; (2) the exposure of the federal taxpayer to losses when program revenues do not cover costs; and (3) the effectiveness, arguably limited, of the nation's floodplain management strategy in reducing federal disaster relief expenditures.

Several lessons emerged from Hurricane Katrina and the 2008 Midwest floods that could help inform Members of the 111th Congress during policy deliberations on the reform and reauthorization of the NFIP.

- **Program Participation to Reduce Uninsured Losses.** Most homeowners do notcompletely recognize or internalize their flood risk and are overly optimisticabout the magnitude of the flood risk to which they are exposed. Consequently,the NFIP has not achieved the level of individual participation originallyenvisioned by Congress. A study of the NFIP's mandatory purchase requirementnationwide conducted by the Rand Corporation indicated that only about 49% ofsingle family homes in SFHA are covered by flood insurance.[18] In the absence offlood insurance, the cost of repairing flood damaged property is usually borneeither by the property owner from their own financial resources, or by federalrelief payments instead of by flood insurance payments. This situation hasresulted in billions of dollars of uninsured property losses and arguably results inhigher social costs. The high degree of uninsured flood losses during the 2008 Midwest floods has raised the policy question of who should appropriately bear the cost of the decision to live in potentially high-risk areas, including areas behind flood control structures.
- **Inadequate Floodplain Management**. The altering of rivers and streams by construction of dams, levees, and other flood control structures arguably increased the risk of major floods and development throughout the affected floodplains. Policymakers learned that there are hidden costs to water resources and flood control structures and that steps must be taken to reduce the risk of future flood disasters. There is the recognition of the need to strengthen the NFIP community land-use and building standards to reduce floodplain development, improve public awareness of flood risk, and reduce cost to U.S. taxpayers. The U.S. Army Corps of Engineers has undertaken cost-benefit analysis of water resources projects. The findings of these studies could be used to better manage the NFIP's floodplain management standards.

- **Flood Risk Assessment and Mapping**. Nationwide actuarial rates and underwriting process may not reflect the actual flood risk in a given location. Property owners affected by Hurricane Katrina and the 2008 Midwest floods may have made location choices that did not consider all of the costs because of inaccurate or outdated flood hazard maps. The price charged for federal flood insurance could understate the risk; premiums may be too low or higher than the actual risk would dictate. Economists note that if property owners had to incur more of the cost of locating in flood-prone areas with the purchase of insurance, they would make more efficient location decisions. Moreover, the maps did not delineate areas of storm water and groundwater flooding or capture increases in localized storm water runoff flooding resulting from development, deforestation, and other land use changes.
- **Residual Risk Behind Levees**. Flood damage in 2008 was relatively high because of the over-reliance on levees and the false sense of security they provide. Homeowners may have thought that because they resided behind a certified levee, they were not subject to flood risk. There are significant potential economic risks of not pricing or establishing sufficient loss reserves to cover residual risks behind flood control structures. Based on the certification of levees as providing at least protection from the 1% annual chance flood, property owners may not be required to purchase flood insurance, yet they may face significant uninsured losses if the levee is overwhelmed. FEMA has consistently sought to communicate to the public the fact that certified levees do not eliminate the risk of flooding. The lack of understanding of the national flood risk, the inadequate communication of that risk, and diminished capabilities in flood risk management due to inaccurate or out-of-date flood hazard maps have been deemed major weaknesses in the program.
- **Inadequate Pricing of Flood Risks**. The most costly flood in the 41-year history of the NFIP was caused not by rainfall-river flooding but by breeched or overtopped levees that did not protect the City of New Orleans from coastal storm surges. According to FEMA, some 75%-80% of the area behind the levees protecting New Orleans was designated SFHA (high-risk zone) due to rainfall and there was an explicit flood insurance purchase requirement in effect in the affected areas. Still, the NFIP assumed the levees were going to hold back

storm surge floods and the program did not adequately price the policies to reflect the possible failure or overtopping of levees.

- **Availability of Federal Disaster Assistance**. Flood victims may have thought, in retrospect correctly, that the purchase of flood insurance was not necessary to receive some compensation for flood related losses from the federal government. The availability of federally-subsidized flood insurance in high-risk areas arguably encouraged too many people to locate in flood-prone areas and to not take appropriate steps to mitigate loss, leaving these financial losses to be either uncompensated or transferred to third-parties, including taxpayers via federal disaster assistance. Economists maintain that the assurance of federal assistance in the event of a repeated disaster creates a "moral hazard" by lowering the incentives to avoid risk. In some ways, this situation arguably counteracts one of the original objectives of the NFIP, namely to minimize future flood damages and the corresponding need for federal disaster relief.

Financial Status

This section examines the current financial status of the program and borrowing from the U.S. Treasury.

Table 2 shows that the NFIP currently has more than 5.6 million policies-in-force nationwide covering approximately $1.19 trillion in property in almost 20,000 participating communities. Policyholders paid $3.1 billion in premiums in 2008. The NFIP experienced only one catastrophic loss year, in 2005, in its 41-year history, and the Midwest floods of 2008 severely tested the financial resiliency of the NFIP. In an attempt to both protect the NFIP's integrity after the 2005 hurricanes and ensure FEMA had the financial resources to cover its existing commitments, Congress passed, and the President signed into law, legislation to increase the NFIP's borrowing authority to allow the agency to continue to pay flood insurance claims: first to $3.5 billion on September 20, 2005; to $18.5 billion on November 21, 2005; and finally to $20.775 billion on March 23, 2006. FEMA had to borrow another $2.6 billion over the 2007 through 2009 period to pay claims from Hurricane Ike and the Midwest floods of 2008. The program's outstanding debt to the Treasury stands at $19.3 billion. FEMA is not likely to be able to repay the debt because of the considerable amount of interest associated with that level of borrowing. Interest payments on the program's debt to the Treasury is almost $1 billion annually.

Table 2. NFIP Program Statistics (as of January 31, 2009; $ Nominal)

Calendar Year	Number of Policies in Force	Total Written Premium	Total Face Value of Coverage	Total Number of Claims Paid	Total Payments Made to Policyholders
1972-1977	NA	NA	NA	4,441	$18,035,656
1978	1,446,354	$111,250,585	$50,500,956,000	29,122	147,719,252
1979	1,843,441	141,535,832	74,375,240,000	71,652	493,008,836
1980	2,103,851	159,009,583	99,259,942,000	41,918	230,414,295
1981	1,915,965	256,798,488	102,059,859,000	23,261	127,118,031
1982	1,900,544	354,842,356	107,296,802,000	32,831	198,295,820
1983	1,981,122	384,225,425	117,834,255,000	51,584	439,454,937
1984	1,926,388	420,530,032	124,421,281,000	27,688	254,642,874
1985	2,016,785	452,466,332	139,948,260,000	38,676	368,238,794
1986	2,119,039	518,226,957	155,717,168,000	13,789	126,388,812
1987	2,115,183	566,391,536	165,953,402,000	13,399	105,422,538
1988	2,149,153	589,453,163	175,764,175,000	7,758	51,022,523
1989	2,292,947	632,204,396	265,218,590,000	36,247	661,668,435
1990	2,477,861	672,791,834	213,588,265,000	14,766	167,919,559
1991	2,532,713	737,078,033	223,098,548,000	28,554	353,684,967
1992	2,623,406	800,973,357	236,844,980,000	44,651	710,247,980
1993	2,828,558	890,425,274	267,870,761,000	36,044	659,069,808
1994	3,040,198	1,003,850,875	295,935,328,000	21,584	411,079,605
1995	3,476,829	1,140,808,119	349,137,768,000	62,441	1,295,581,467
1996	3,693,076	1,275,176,752	400,681,650,000	52,679	828,040,301
1997	4,102,416	1,509,787,517	462,606,433,000	30,338	519,505,659
1998	4,235,138	1,668,246,681	497,621,083,000	57,349	886,305,129
1999	4,329,986	1,719,652,696	534,117,781,000	47,246	754,971,355
2000	4,369,087	1,723,824,570	567,568,653,000	16,362	251,719,208
2001	4,458,470	1,740,331,079	611,918,920,000	43,588	1,276,986,570
2002	4,519,799	1,802,277,937	653,776,126,000	25,314	433,634,571
2003	4,565,491	1,897,687,479	691,786,140,000	36,833	779,908,320
2004	4,667,446	2,040,828,486	765,205,681,000	55,762	2,226,942,412
2005	4,962,011	2,241,264,140	876,679,658,000	211,954	17,646,657,418
2006	5,517,089	2,615,890,367	1,054,087,148,000	24,562	638,824,231
2007	5,653,949	2,854,071,096	1,139,822,517,000	23,003	$607,055,453
2008	5,610,895	$3,074,184,710	1,185,136,863,800	69,466	$3,045,743,940

Source: U.S. Department of Homeland Security, Federal Emergency Management Agency's Office of Legislative Affairs.

Table 3. History of U.S.Treasury Borrowing under the National Flood Insurance Program (as of March 31, 2010; $ Nominal)

Fiscal Year	Amount Borrowed	Amount Repaid	Cumulative Debt
Prior to FY1981[a]	$917,406,008	$0	$917,406,088
1981	164,614,526	624,970,009	457,050,435
1982	13,915,000	470,965,435	0
1983	50,000,000	0	50,000,000
1984[b]	200,000,000	36,879,123	213,120,877
1985	0	213,120,877	0
1994[c]	100,000,000	100,000,000	0
1995	265,000,000	0	265,000,000
1996	423,600,000	62,000,000	626,600,000
1997	530,000,000	239,600,000	917,000,000
1998	0	395,000,000	522,000,000
1999	400,000,000	381,000,000	541,000,000
2000	345,000,000	541,000,000	345,000,000
2001	600,000,000	345,000,000	600,000,000
2002	50,000,000	640,000,000	10,000,000
October 2001	0	10,000,000	0
2003 (Nov.-Sept.)	0	0	0
2004	0	0	0
2005[d]	300,000,000	75,000,000	225,000,000
2006	16,660,000,000	0	16,885,000,000
2007	650,000,000	0	17,535,000,000
2008	50,000,000	225,000,000	17,360,000,000
2009	1,987,988,421	347,988,421	19,000,000,000
2010 to date	0	250,000,000	18,750,000,000
Total	23,707,523,955	4,957,523,955	18,750,000,000

Source: U.S. Department of Homeland Security, Federal Emergency Management Agency's Office of Legislative Affairs.

Notes: Borrowings through 1985 were repaid from congressional appropriations. Borrowings since 1994 have been repaid from premium and other income.

a. Balance forward from U.S. Department of Housing and Urban Development.

b. Figure for the $213.1 million in cumulative debt in 1984 provided by FEMA reflects additional cost outside of the insurance program.

c. Of the $100 million borrowed, only $11 million was needed to cover obligations.

d. NFIP borrowed $300 million in 2005 to pay claims from the 2004 hurricane season, but Hurricanes Katrina, Rita and Wilma struck on August 29, 2005 and claims were submitted after the 2006 fiscal year began.

NFIP Treasury Borrowing

Table 3 shows the history of U.S. Treasury borrowing and repayments under the NFIP from 1981 to 2009. The NFIP was self-supporting from 1986 until 2005, covering all administrative expenses and claim payments out of premium income and fees. Since Hurricane Katrina struck in August 2005, FEMA has had to borrow $19.3 billion, which includes amounts to pay claims from Hurricanes Ike and the 2008 Midwest floods. It is unlikely that the $19.3 billion Treasury debt will be repaid within the next 10 years given annual interest payments of about $900 million and annual premium income of approximately $3.1 billion. Experts agree that even if FEMA increased flood insurance rates up to the maximum amount allowed by law (10% per year), the program would still not have sufficient funds to cover future obligations for policyholder claims, operating expenses, and interest on debt.

Factors Affecting Financial Solvency

Homeowners are required to purchase flood insurance coverage if they have a federally insured mortgage. Many policyholders, however, cancel their NFIP policy after a few years pass and they have not experienced a flood loss. As a result, when the flood hazard does occur, there are a large number of uninsured flood victims and the federal government is usually called upon to provide disaster assistance. In order to stabilize future government spending to compensate flood victims, it is important to maintain the long-term financial solvency of the NFIP. In considering the NFIP's financial solvency, one should recognize two things: (1) the NFIP was not capitalized at inception by Congress; and (2) the program does not operate under the traditional insurance definition of fiscal solvency that requires the insurer to have sufficient capital/surplus to obtain authorization to sell insurance policies.

With respect to the financial solvency of the NFIP, several issues are of concern to Congress, including the following:

- flood insurance premium discount (i.e., actuarial soundness and premium rateadequacy);
- repetitive loss properties' disproportionate share of total losses in the program;

- lack of enforcement of mandatory flood insurance purchase require-ements;
- impact of outdated flood maps on the program;
- enforcement of floodplain management regulations; and
- debate over the inclusion of optional windstorm coverage in the NFIP policy.

The next six sections examines each of these concerns.

Flood Insurance Premium Discounts

The NFIP arguably faces a long-term solvency challenge because the program does not have a financing mechanism for handling catastrophic losses other than borrowing from the federal Treasury; annual premiums are not likely to cover the program's long-term expenses, claim costs, and interest and principal debt repayment to the U.S. Treasury. Taxpayers could therefore be exposed to greater financial risks as a result of the potential for future catastrophic flooding.[19]

NFIP was not established on an actuarially sound basis since it charges less-than actuarial rates for pre-FIRM structures. FEMA's rate-setting structure is designed to generate premiums at least sufficient to cover losses and loss adjustment expenses relative to the "historical average loss year."[20] There is no contingent amount added to premium for profit margins in order to build a surplus. When losses and expenses exceed premiums the program is authorized to borrow from the U.S. Treasury but must repay the funds with interest. Thus, because the program does not build loss reserves for the infrequent but very catastrophic loss years and rates are by statute underpriced to make rates affordable, the program's financial structure could impose negative externalities on taxpayers. Federal taxpayers ultimately subsidize any financial shortfalls created by the NFIP's financial structure and the tendency to underprice the insurance coverage.

The NFIP uses a two-tier rate classification system that consists of "actuarial" rates and "subsidized" rates.[21] Actuarial flood insurance premiums are calculated based on the amount of coverage, location, age, and building occupancy and, for a building in a SFHA, the elevation of the building. Based on expected losses derived from flood probability estimates and adding expected loss adjustments and other operating expenses (i.e., risk loading), FEMA is able to calculate an actuarial rate. Buildings constructed after December 31, 1974 or after the publication of a flood insurance rate map

(FIRM) are charged an actuarial premium that reflects the property's risk of flooding.

Subsidized rates, on the other hand, are determined by a statutory mandate that requires rates to be affordable so individuals are encouraged to participate. Owners of properties built prior to the issuance of a community's flood hazard map or January 1, 1974, usually pay subsidized rates and are exempted from the NFIP's floodplain management standards. Even properties that are remapped into higher-risk areas pay the subsidized rates, which further contributes to the financial inadequacies of the NFIP.

Premium subsidies were initially considered necessary because occupants often did not understand the flood risk when they built in floodplains (flood maps were not available), there were no public safeguards prohibiting the occupancy on the floodplain, and premium subsidies on pre-FIRM structures could provide an incentive to local communities to participate in the program and discourage unwise future floodplains construction. Premium subsidies were intended to be phased out over time as the number of pre-FIRM properties gradually diminished when they were damaged and rebuilt or relocated under stronger floodplain management and building codes. The NFIP requires all new and substantially improved buildings to be constructed at or above the elevation of the 1%-annual-chance flood (100-year floodplain).

Repetitive Flood Loss Properties

Properties that experience repetitive flood losses, known as a "repetitive-loss properties" (RLP) and "severe repetitive loss properties"(SRLP), account for a disproportionately large share of all the flood insurance claims filed and paid under the NFIP.[22] Historically, it is estimated that approximately 1% of the properties insured under the NFIP have accounted for over a third of claims paid. About one in 10 homes that suffer repetitive flood damages have cumulative flood insurance claims that have exceeded the value of the house.[23] FEMA approximates that 90% of all RLPs were built prior to December 31, 1974, or before the adoption of a FIRM—and, hence, are subject to premium discounts.[24] Importantly, the annual increase in new RLPs is outpacing FEMA mitigation efforts by a factor of 10 to 1.[25] After the 1993 Midwest flood, FEMA and other federal government agencies spent hundreds of millions to remove frequently flooded properties from the floodplain.

Table 4.Total Repetitive Flood Loss Properties in the NFIP: 1978 - 2009 (as of February 28, 2009; $ Nominal)

Building Payments	$7,686,059,344
Contents Payments	$2,424,908,942
Total payments	$10,110,968,286
Average payment	$23,591
Losses	428,583
Properties	148,148

Source: U.S. Department of Homeland Security, Federal Emergency Management Agency.

Table 4 shows that since 1978, a total of 148,148 RLPs have had 428,583 claims paid, which have cost the National Flood Insurance Fund a total of $10.1 billion in nominal dollars. Table A-1 shows RLPs by state. The average claim for these properties was $23,591. According to FEMA, there were 8,909 insured SRLP and 71,680 insured RLPs in the NFIP, as of February 28, 2009. The agency awarded $34.9 million to mitigate 168 properties under the SRLP program and $28.1 million under the Repetitive Flood Claims program. The Inspector General at the Department of Homeland Security estimates that it would cost about $1.8 billion to mitigate the current inventory of SRLP.[26]

FEMA has undertaken several actions over the years to address the RLP problem. The initial strategy, announced in 1999, was to identify the nation's inventory of RLPs and focus on structures that were substantially damaged (i.e., damaged 50% or more of market value) at which time they would be reconstructed, elevated, or floodproofed to prevent future damage. One reported difficulty has been reluctance and inconsistency at the local community level in declaring structures substantially damaged.

FEMA also pursued a strategy of phasing out premium subsidies on RLPs through voluntary buyouts or the imposition of full actuarially based rates for RLP owners who refuse to accept FEMA's offer to mitigate the effect of flood damage. In addition, the agency incorporated special incentives into the Community Rating System and provided data to states and communities to help them address the RLPs.

The Flood Insurance Reform Act of 2004 required FEMA to establish the Repetitive Flood Claims and the Severe Repetitive Loss Grant programs to provide funding to reduce or eliminate the long-term risk of flood damage under the NFIP. The RFC grant program provides grants to help states provide subgrants to local government to acquire properties and either demolish or relocate the structure, or elevate or otherwise floodproof the structure. Congress has appropriated $10 million annually to the RFC grant program since 2006. Going forward, a policy challenge will be to find a way to mitigate RLP given that FEMA cannot directly compel property owners in flood hazard areas to mitigate losses or impose actuarial rates on RLP.

Mandatory Flood Insurance Purchase Requirement

FEMA lacks nationwide data on the number of properties in floodplains: it is therefore difficult to make an accurate assessment of NFIP market penetration. However, estimates of penetration rates in the 100-year floodplain are arguably consistently low. A 2006 Rand Corporation study estimated that about 49% of properties in SFHAs purchased NFIP flood insurance, and 1% of properties outside SFHAs purchased insurance.[27] Concerns have also been expressed about the large number of homes that are not mortgaged and thus are not required to be insured against flood risks. The low participation rates in flood-prone areas may be of concern to Congress.

The intent and success of the NFIP rests on making insurance widely available and property owners and renters purchasing coverage. Since 1973, federal regulations have required flood insurance on all structures located in the 1% annual chance floodplain (100-year floodplain). Also, since 1994, recipients of certain flood disaster assistance have been required to purchase and hold flood insurance to protect against future flood losses, under penalty of receiving no federal disaster aid in subsequent floods.[28] Despite the existence of this mandatory flood insurance purchase requirement, take-up rates for flood insurance have historically been low and the federal government's exposure to uninsured property losses from flooding remains substantial. There are at least five possible explanations for the low market penetration for flood insurance: (1) flood insurance is not seen as being worth the cost (i.e., a poor investment); (2) the individual has misperceptions about low-probability risks and lacks information about the NFIP;[29] (3) private insurance agents do not market NFIP policies; (4) lack of compliance with the mandatory purchase requirement or failure to ensure that property owners maintain coverage for the life of the loan; (5) many homeowners in risky areas either do not have a mortgage or have a mortgage from an unregulated lender that is not subject to the mandatory purchase requirement.

Flood Hazard Mapping

FEMA is required by statute to identify and map the nation's floodplain areas and to establish flood-risk zones in such areas. FIRMs are used for setting flood insurance rates, regulating floodplain development and communicating information about the 1%-annual-chance flood hazard to those who live in floodplains. FIRMs also are used to determine whether property owners are required by law to obtain flood insurance as a condition of obtaining mortgage loans or other federally related financial assistance. Without accurate and updated flood hazard maps, property owners and small businesses could underestimate their exposure to flood risks and make poor financial decisions about protecting their properties (i.e., where to build and whether to purchase flood insurance or take other measures to protect their properties).

A major challenge facing the NFIP is ensuring the accuracy of the nation's inventory of FIRMS and improving the mapping, communication, and management of flood-related data. Other flood risk assessment and mapping issues that may be of concern to Congress include (1) the sudden inclusion in a floodplain that can result from FEMA Map Modernization program; (2) large areas that appear to be outside of SFHA that should actuarially be in the high-hazard area; (3) hazard mitigation and local planning for capital investments behind suspect levees and below aging dams so property owners will continue to be exempt from the mandatory purchase requirements;(4) expiring Provisional Accredited levee agreements; and (5) certification/liability issues with levee-like structures.[30]

When FEMA's map modernization program began in 2003, nearly 70% of the nation's 92,222 flood maps were more than 10 years old and many of these maps did not reflect the current flood hazard risk or new estimation techniques. In many cases, water flow and drainage patterns have changed due to surface erosion, land use and natural forces. The probability of inland and riverine flooding in certain areas has changed along with these factors. Most experts agree that flood maps with high-accuracy and high-resolution land surface elevation data would be helpful. The benefits of accurate flood hazard maps include improved risk zone designations as well as insurance premiums and building restrictions that reflect actual flood risks facing individuals and businesses.

The Map Modernization program called for FEMA to produce a new nationwide Flood Insurance Study (FIS) and the accompanying FIRMs.[31] FEMA is now completing the update and conversion to digital food hazard maps using new technologies such as Light Detection And Ranging (LiDAR) and other remote sensing technologies within a geographic information system (GIS) format to systematically update floodplain maps on a watershed scale.

Any community that currently participates in the NFIP, or is now identified as having flood hazard prone areas in the FIS and on the new FIRMs, must officially adopt the county-wide FIS and the accompanying FIRMs. Such official action is the most critical community action that FEMA requires of all communities having flood hazard prone areas. Any participating community failing to meet the FEMA map adoption deadline faces immediate suspension or sanctions from the NFIP.

In October 2008, FEMA announced the discontinuation of the paper FIRMS, flood insurance study (FIS) reports, and related flood hazard map products.[32] Only digital map images and digital geospatial flood hazard data will be distributed by FEMA and are equivalent to the paper maps for official activities under the NFIP. The paper maps will still be available through the FEMA Map Service Center. This change is expected to result in printing and distribution cost savings for FEMA during the map modernization process by eliminating the need to generate large format film negatives to support offset printing.[33] FEMA has also announced its Risk Mapping, Assessment, and Planning Strategy aims to follow-up to the Map Modernization initiative. The new strategy aims to combine flood hazard mapping, risk assessment tools, and mitigation planning into one seamless program.

Floodplain Management Regulations

FEMA is prohibited from providing flood insurance to property owners residing in communities that do not participate in the NFIP.[34] Local communities must adopt and enforce certain minimum floodplain management ordinances as a condition of participation in the NFIP. FEMA estimates that $1.2 billion in flood losses are avoided each year from community floodplain management requirements. Efforts to guide construction and development away from high-risk areas through community-based land use and zoning ordinances, however, have reportedly been subordinated to building and elevation requirements that lead to further development of the floodplains, according to the National Wildlife Federation.[35] Even in hazard-prone floodways and coastal areas, building and rebuilding are allowed under NFIP standards, with the cost of insurance varying with property elevation.

An important floodplain management issue for the 111th Congress is reconciling FEMA's implementation of its policy on federal assistance for recovery and hazard mitigation projects located in coastal velocity zones—the so-called V zones on FIRMS—with that of other federal departments and agencies charged with implementing Executive Order 11988.[36] President Jimmy Carter signed into law E.O. 11988 to require federal agencies to avoid direct and indirect support of floodplain development by taking action "to reduce the risk of flood loss, to minimize the impact of floods on human safety, health and welfare, and to restore and preserve the natural and beneficial values served by floodplains in carrying out its responsibilities."[37]

Although the regulatory guidelines for E.O. 11988 are clearly outlined in 44 CFR Part 9, there have been inconsistencies and uncertainty in interpreting those guidelines to determine whether officials are to support recovery and community development in V Zones. FEMA staff must (1) determine eligibility and required elevation of all new construction in coastal high hazard areas on the Gulf Coast; and (2) decide whether new structures or the costs of repair or replacement of facilities in V Zones are eligible for FEMA funding. The decision to approve and obligate FEMA recovery funds for public assistance projects located in V Zones is an essential element in the reconstruction or redevelopment of coastal areas devastated by Hurricane Katrina.

Federal Multi-Peril Insurance Program

In the aftermath of Hurricanes Katrina and Rita, individuals and businesses in Louisiana, Mississippi, and Alabama protested against what they claimed were inappropriate obstacles to the payment of their property damage insurance claims. When insurance adjustors and damage experts assessed the properties damaged by Hurricane Katrina, they were faced with the issue of allocating damages between wind (a covered loss) and flood (an excluded loss). Post-Katrina insurance claims litigation and the delays and economic uncertainty generated for consumers and insurers raised concerns about post-event judicial interpretations of the scope of insurance coverage.[38]

One issue of contention that emerged from the wind vs. water claims dispute was the interest in expanding the NFIP to allow policyholders to purchase optional wind coverage. In the 110th Congress, the House passed H.R. 3121, the Flood Insurance Reform and Modernization Act, in 2007, that included an amendment offered by Representative Gene Taylor to expand the NFIP to include wind damage insurance. When the Senate Banking Committee reported the Senate companion bill, S. 2284, the legislation did not include the Taylor Amendment. No further action occurred on either bill.

Proponents of adding the wind peril provision argue it is necessary to eliminate coverage disputes when wind and flood both contribute to a loss. Optional wind coverage is also said to be needed because of the difficulty that property owners have in obtaining affordable private wind coverage in states along the Gulf and Atlantic coasts. Private insurers have dramatically increased premiums and deductibles, reduced coverage or withdrawn altogether from these areas out of concern about catastrophic risk exposure. In those areas, homeowners must instead purchase their wind coverage from state pools, where the premiums can be prohibitively expensive.

Opponents of adding wind coverage to the NFIP believe that there is adequate wind coverage capacity in every state through either the traditional private market or through the state residual market program (e.g., wind pools). Some critics of the optional wind proposal would instead like to see the development of federal programs to provide economic incentives to encourage the adoption and enforcement of stronger building codes and other loss mitigation efforts. According to these critics, expanding the NFIP to add wind coverage would dramatically increase the exposure of the NFIP, losses to the federal government and the potential for huge taxpayer subsidies. Concerns have also been expressed about the NFIP's ability to determine actuarially sound rates for the windstorm portion of this coverage and avoid wide-scale financial deficits in the program following a catastrophic flood event. Even if actuarial rates are implemented they may not produce sufficient premium income to bear program administration costs and losses in the event of a catastrophic event.

The Government Accountability Office (GAO) issued a recent report that outlined some difficulties that FEMA could face in implementing an optional wind coverage provision. Some of the obstacles included (1) the concern about "adverse selection" or the likelihood that only those property owners at highest risk would purchase coverage; (2) wind hazard prevention standards that communities would have to adopt in order to receive coverage; (3) uncertainty about the adoption of programs to accommodate wind coverage; (4) difficulties in establishing a new rate setting process; (5) enforcement of new building codes; and (6) administration and oversight of the program.

A letter to President Barack Obama from a coalition of consumer, insurance and reinsurance groups outlined a different approach to the insurance availability and conflict of interest concerns. The coalition supports the creation of a bipartisan Commission on Natural Catastrophe Risk Management and Insurance that consist of experts in areas such as insurance, reinsurance, policyholder concerns, risk mitigation, public finance, flood hazard mapping, building standards, emergency management and environmental issues.[39] The Obama Administration has expressed opposition to adding wind coverage to the NFIP based on the arguments that coverage was available in the private sector and through state-sponsored wind pools.

Options for Managing and Financing Flood Risk

Despite investing significant resources in managing flood risk and minimizing future disaster relief costs, the United States has not been able to curb the rising costs of flood damage. This was the conclusion of the Gilbert F. White National Flood Policy Forum held in November 2007 at George Washington University. The Forum brought together 92 diverse experts to consider the future of floodplain management under a "business-as-usual scenario" and under an alternative scenario of aggressive action to address increasing flood risk in the Nation. The experts at the forum concluded that (1) an unprecedented set of conditions (e.g., population growth and migration, changes in climate, and degradation of water-based resources) now face the United States that could increase flood losses more rapidly in the near future; and (2) existing programs and policies at all levels are short-sighted, fragmented, focused on economic development at the expense of sustainability and that future losses must be managed more pro-actively than in the past.

What should the policy response be to the current financial and management challenges facing the NFIP? There are five main policy options.

- **Reform and modernize the NFIP**. Reform of the NFIP could include (1) a gradual phase in of actuarial rates for non-residential properties, non-primaryresidences and RLPs; (2) strengthening floodplain management regulationsdesigned to restrict development in high-risk areas, and require new constructionto be elevated three feet above the base flood elevation (BFE); (3) authorizing anongoing program to review, update, and maintain flood insurance program mapsand include 500-year floodplains and areas that are behind levees, downstream ofa dam, or in a coastal area that could see a major hurricane; (4) strengthening andenforcing mandatory insurance purchase requirements; (5) forgiving the full debtowed by the NFIP to the Treasury; (6) eliminating the current subsidy for olderstructures and expand to include areas where a flood or storm surge is likely if aweather event reaches catastrophic levels; (7) creating a catastrophe reserve fundfor extremely rare catastrophic loss years; and (8) encouraging private sectorincentives for participation.
- **Long-term flood insurance contracts** (LTFI) coupled with mitigation loans arguably would encourage investment in risk-reduction measures.[40] The idea is for private insurers to offer 5-, 10-, or 20-year flood insurance contracts combined with long-term

mitigation loans (e.g., for retrofitting, elevation, and floodproofing of structures) tied to the mortgage. Mitigation loans would be offered to help finance the high upfront costs associated with investing in mitigation measures. The long-term flood insurance policies would have a maturity that corresponds to the length of the mortgage on the property and the policy would not terminate when the property owner sells the property.

The economic rationale for using LTFI to pre-fund disaster costs is that insurers, generally, need guaranteed premiums for a long time period if rates are to be based on expected losses. By lengthening the term of the property insurance contract, and spreading the risk through a mandatory purchase requirement, LTFI contracts could implicitly permit insurers to compensate for their present inability to prepare adequately for rare and unpredictable flood events.

- **Shift flood insurance back into the private sector.** FEMA has a responsibility to examine the NFIP's contingent liabilities and recommend ways to provide financial stability to the federal flood insurance program. This activity is performed in conjunction with the program's annual rate-setting process. Recognizing the shortcomings of the current financing arrangement, two basic alternatives have emerged: an all-hazard insurance approach and a federal-insurance (reinsurance) framework that would enable private insurers to cover more flood risks.

  With the development of computer simulation catastrophe risk models and remote sensing technologies, some private insurers have argued that flood hazards are now insurable by private companies working in partnership with government. Some economists have suggested that floods and other catastrophic risks are now insurable because of insurer's ability to transfer catastrophic risks to the capital markets through securitization of the risk. In this context, FEMA could require private insurers to "make available" private flood insurance policies at actuarially determined prices in flood-prone areas with the federal government providing federal reinsurance. FEMA could also open the NFIP to a competitive bid contractor to have one firm take over the entire Write-Your-Own program and the government reinsure the risk. In 2000, FEMA undertook a study to explore alternative financing arrangements to reduce the need for U.S. Treasury borrowing. FEMA was concerned about the NFIP's erratic cash flow and the potential for catastrophic losses within a short period of time. The option that received the most attention was to create a reinsurance vehicle to finance catastrophic losses. After review by the Office of Management and Budget (OMB), this option was not adopted because it was determined that the cost to borrow from the U.S. Treasury was lower.

- **Community Group Flood Insurance Policy.** The local community purchases a group policy from the NFIP on behalf of residents in a designated SFHA. Policies are issued to all residents and paid either through property taxes or as a utility payment. Professor Dwight Jaffee at Berkley and Howard Kunreuther at the Wharton School are the leading advocates for the long-term flood insurance contract proposal.[41]
- **Interstate Compacts for Flood Control and Management.** In response to recurring flooding on the Red River, Members of the 111th Congress may wish to consider addressing the long-term flooding challenges facing residences along the Red River Valley. One way to do this would be to create a Red River Valley Interstate Compact Authority with the power to address water quality and flooding issues in the Red River watershed. This could serve as a model for the nation. Officials from North Dakota, South Dakota, and Minnesota envision this entity as an efficient and cost-effective approach to handling the high cost of maintaining dams and levees, land purchases for water retention, diversion of the river, and reducing the time it takes to complete water management projects. Before the request for an interstate compact is presented to Congress, the state legislatures in North Dakota, South Dakota and Minnesota would need to approve separate resolutions to set up the compact. The status quo is an ad hoc approach with multiple states each responding to its own flood hazards and the federal government providing post-disaster relief assistance.

APPENDIX. NATIONAL FLOOD INSURANCE PROGRAM: REPETITIVE FLOOD LOSS PROPERTIES (AS OF FEBRUARY 28, 2009; $ NOMINAL)

Table A-1. Repetitive Flood Loss Properties in the National Flood Insurance Program (as of February 28, 2009; $ Nominal)

State Name	Building Payments	Contents Payments	Total Payments	Average Payment	Losses	Properties
Alabama	$393,092,368.03	$79,103,294.37	$472,195,662.40	$35,296.43	13,378	4,746
Alaska	670,015.90	111,023.15	781,039.05	11,833.93	66	26
Arizona	6,416,295.62	1,301,575.04	7,717,870.66	13,708.47	563	245
Arkansas	14,589,085.43	6,300,487.87	20,889,573.30	15,270.16	1,368	492
California	149,890,383.20	36,748,972.80	186,639,356.00	21,015.58	8,881	3,247
Colorado	907,408.11	334,172.67	1,241,580.78	10,094.15	123	53
Connecticut	46,440,356.38	16,646,881.12	63,087,237.50	15,436.07	4,087	1,384
Delaware	21,147,972.41	12,319,920.72	33,467,893.13	35,794.54	935	345
District Columbia	581,743.34	16,919.85	598,663.19	20,643.56	29	12
Florida	1,027,255,883.88	273,673,719.91	1,300,929,603.79	32,092.40	40,537	16,061
Georgia	57,145,015.84	16,618,640.44	73,763,656.28	22,144.60	3,331	1,233
Guam	350,626.18	52,467.45	403,093.63	13,899.78	29	14
Hawaii	9,493,533.40	2,199,862.67	11,693,396.07	24,669.61	474	170
Idaho	577,539.26	99,298.69	676,837.95	11,280.63	60	24

Table A-1. (Continued)

State Name	Building Payments	Contents Payments	Total Payments	Average Payment	Losses	Properties
Illinois	97,910,660.14	23,307,974.88	121,218,635.02	11,716.47	10,346	3,440
Indiana	40,998,960.41	8,932,887.22	49,931,847.63	14,972.07	3,335	1,235
Iowa	39,851,921.99	8,898,364.76	48,750,286.75	21,131.46	2,307	907
Kansas	16,659,677.66	8,865,407.37	25,525,085.03	22,118.79	1,154	419
Kentucky	64,297,899.14	21,745,431.94	86,043,331.08	17,520.53	4,911	1,527
Louisiana	1,894,665,529.35	607,625,788.56	2,502,291,317.91	26,854.09	93,181	29,446
Maine	8,931,382.07	2,699,006.41	11,630,388.48	20,332.85	572	218
Maryland	38,362,365.25	14,378,881.58	52,741,246.83	26,397.02	1,998	851
Massachusetts	108,577,982.61	23,592,910.05	132,170,892.66	17,054.31	7,750	2,727
Michigan	11,138,124.96	4,672,158.33	15,810,283.29	10,347.04	1,528	596
Minnesota	18,346,566.93	3,042,146.81	21,388,713.74	15,299.51	1,398	573
Mississippi	418,196,518.64	124,798,955.97	542,995,474.61	32,686.94	16,612	5,842
Missouri	180,591,223.32	87,915,249.57	268,506,472.89	16,390.34	16,382	4,770
Montana	789,889.65	114,904.58	904,794.23	9,327.78	97	44
Nebraska	6,724,661.79	2,592,140.92	9,316,802.71	11,293.09	825	335
Nevada	6,955,145.75	3,436,879.89	10,392,025.64	59,383.00	175	76
New Hampshire	14,879,929.25	2,330,394.65	17,210,323.90	22,645.16	760	312
New Jersey	369,238,723.50	139,422,392.12	508,661,115.62	17,947.89	28,341	9,273
New Mexico	1,101,361.25	49,475.85	1,150,837.10	13,228.01	87	38
New York	224,708,052.65	79,949,917.08	304,657,969.73	13,524.73	22,526	8,314

Table A-1. (Continued)

State Name	Building Payments	Contents Payments	Total Payments	Average Payment	Losses	Properties
North Carolina	333,459,846.73	58,225,499.25	391,685,345.98	19,388.44	20,202	7,483
North Dakota	10,321,744.29	1,518,550.88	11,840,295.17	23,492.65	504	224
Ohio	68,745,492.09	23,561,189.40	92,306,681.49	17,612.42	5,241	1,921
Oklahoma	42,380,779.14	13,113,203.88	55,493,983.02	19,024.33	2,917	908
Oregon	16,407,790.89	5,453,937.15	21,861,728.04	25,332.25	863	336
Pennsylvania	315,625,689.09	101,863,089.77	417,488,778.86	24,377.48	17,126	6,389
Puerto Rico	14,646,719.93	37,255,363.89	51,902,083.82	8,748.03	5,933	2,072
Rhode Island	10,400,456.25	8,187,606.70	18,588,062.95	29,089.30	639	213
South Carolina	69,062,474.30	15,315,615.75	84,378,090.05	23,091.98	3,654	1,459
South Dakota	2,307,168.13	399,432.09	2,706,600.22	15,205.62	178	83
Tennessee	21,169,718.05	9,375,910.38	30,545,628.43	14,069.84	2,171	753
Texas	1,175,308,859.37	425,712,661.54	1,601,021,520.91	26,408.17	60,626	19,496
Utah	895,525.28	202,236.88	1,097,762.16	18,296.04	60	24
Vermont	1,491,997.34	537,561.24	2,029,558.58	13,530.39	150	64
Virgin Islands	11,595,843.24	18,351,300.44	29,947,143.68	46,357.81	646	246
Virginia	135,343,012.55	38,198,691.25	173,541,703.80	22,415.62	7,742	2,965
Washington	65,556,993.36	13,420,570.92	78,977,564.28	24,211.39	3,262	1,136
West Virginia	82,966,263.98	36,112,490.50	119,078,754.48	16,529.53	7,204	2,806
Wisconsin	16,681,900.28	4,174,490.83	20,856,391.11	16,080.49	1,297	565
Wyoming	206,266.45	31,034.15	237,300.60	10,786.39	22	9
Total	$7,686,059,344.03	$2,424,908,942.18	$10,110,968,286.21	$23,591.62	428,583	148,148

Source: U.S. Department of Homeland Security, Federal Emergency Management Agency.

End Notes

[1] In 2004, Congress passed the *Bunning-Bereuter-Blumenauer Flood Insurance Reform Act* to reauthorize the NFIP through September 30, 2008 (P.L. 108-264; 118 Stat. 712). On September 30, 2008, President George W. Bush signed into law H.R. 2638, the Consolidated Security, Disaster Assistance, and Continuing Appropriations Act of 2009 (P.L. 110-329; 122 Stat. 3575, 3581), that included a provision to extend the NFIP's authority to issue new policies, increase coverage on existing policies, and issue renewal policies until March 6, 2009. After approving a five-day continuing resolution that Congress passed and President Barack Obama signed into law on March 6, 2009 (P.L. 111-6; 123 Stat 522), Congress passed the Omnibus Appropriations Act of 2009, extending the NFIP through September 30, 2009 (P.L. 111-8; 123 Stat. 988). On July 29, 2009, the House considered and passed H.R. 3139 under suspension of the rules to reauthorize the NFIP through March 6, 2010. On March 2, 2010, Congress passed and the President signed into law H.R. 4691, which extended the NFIP through March 28, 2010. On April 15, Congress passed P.L. 111-157 to extend the program to May 31, 2010. On July 2, 2010, President Obama signed into law H.R. 5569 (P.L. 111-196) to extend the program through September 30, 2010.

[2] P.L. 111-196; 124 Stat. 1352.

[3] 42 U.S.C. § 4012a.

[4] *U.S. Department of Homeland Security, Federal Emergency Management Agency*, "Memorandum on Lapse in NFIP Authority, FEMA," May 28, 2010, located at http://www.fema.gov/pdf/nfip/w_10063.pdf.

[5] *Federal Reserve Board*, "Informal Guidance on the lapse of FEMA's Authority to Issue Flood Insurance Contracts," March 29, 2010, available at http://www.federalreserve.gov/boarddocs/caletters/2010/1003/10-3-attachment.pdf; *Office of Controller of the Currency*, "Guidance Regarding Lapse and Extension of FEMA's Authority to Issue Flood Insurance Contracts," located at http://www.occ.treas.gov/ftp/ bulletin/2010-20.html; and *Fannie Mae*, "Fannie to Continue Buying Loans During Lapse of Flood Insurance," available at http://www.housingwire.com/2010/04/02/ fannie-to-continue-buying-loans-during-lapse-of-flood-insurance.

[6] *Office of Comptroller of the Currency*, *OCC Bulletin OCC 2010-20*, "Guidance Regarding Lapse and Extension of FEMA's Authority to Issue Flood Insurance Contracts," June 9, 2010, located at http://www.occ.treas.gov/ftp/bulletin/ 2010-20.html.

[7] 42 U.S.C. 4012a.

[8] *Fannie Mae*, "Fannie to Continue Buying Loans During Lapse of Flood Insurance," available at http://www.housingwire.com/2010/04/02/fannie-to-continue-buying-loans-during-lapse-of-flood-insurance.

[9] National Science and Technology Council, Climate Change Science Program and the Subcommittee on Global Change Research, *Weather and Climate Extremes in a Changing Climate -Regions of Focus: North America, Hawaii, Caribbean, and U.S. Pacific Islands*, June 2008, at http://www.climatescience.gov/Library/sap/sap3-3/final-report/ sap3-3-final-all.pdf.

[10] U.S. Commission on Ocean Policy, *An Ocean Blueprint for the 21St Century*, September 2004, at http://oceancommission.gov/documents/full_color_rpt/000_ocean_full_report.pdf.

[11] Lloyds of London and Risk Management Solutions, *Coastal Communities and Climate Change: Maintaining Insurability*, 2008, at http://www.lloyds.com/NR/rdonlyres/ 38782611-5ED3-4FDC-85A4-5DEAA88A2DA0/0/FINAL360climatechangereport.pdf.

[12] James Anderson, "Economic Regulation," *Encyclopedia of Policy Studies*, Stuart S. Nagel, ed. (New York; Dekker Publishers), 1994, p. 404.

[13] Dan R. Anderson, The National Flood Insurance Program: Problem and Potential, *The Journal of Risk and Insurance*, 1974, vol.16 (4), p. 579-599.

[14] Flood damage reduction is thought to be achievable through extensive flood control structures, such as levees and dams and non-structural methods, including land use ordinances, buy-outs, and elevation of existing buildings and roads.

[15] P.L. 93-234, 87 Stat 975.

[16] P.L. 103-325, 108 Stat. 2255.

[17] P.L. 108-264, 118 Stat. 712.

[18] Rand Institute for Civil Justice, "The National Flood Insurance Program's Market Penetration Rate: Estimates and Policy Implications," http://www.rand.org/pubs/technical_reports/2006/RAND_TR300.pdf.

[19] U.S. Government Accountability Office, *FEMA's Rate-Setting Process Warrants Attention*, GAO-09-12, Oct. 31, 2008.

[20] In contrast, commercial insurance premiums are typically set at a level that covers expected losses and expenses plus an amount for a profit margin. A portion of each premium dollar collected is then set aside in loss reserves which are invested and the income used to pay claims and expenses.

[21] A third category of premium discounts involve "grandfathered" policies that occur when a structure is built in compliance with the local floodplain regulation in effect at the time of construction but is later placed in a different risk zone when a flood map is changed. The structure is grandfathered so that pre-FIRM structures continue to pay the subsidized rates.

[22] A repetitive loss property (RLP) is defined as an insured property that experiences two or more flood losses greater than $1,000 within any 10-year period. A subset of RLPs, called severe repetitive loss properties (SRLP), have incurred at least four NFIP claim payments of at least $5,000 each or the cumulative amount of such claims payments exceeds $20,000 or for which at least two separate claims have been made with the cumulative amount of the building portion of such claims exceeding the market value of the building.

[23] U.S. Department of Homeland Security, Office of Inspector General, "FEMA's Implementation of the Flood Insurance Reform Act of 2004," OIG-09-45, March 26, 2009, p. 4, at http://www.dhs.gov/xoig/assets/mgmtrpts/ OIG_09-45_Mar09.pdf.

[24] Ibid.

[25] Ibid, p. 13.

[26] *DHS Inspector General Report*, p. 1.

[27] Rand Institute for Civil Justice, "The National Flood Insurance Program's Market Penetration Rate: Estimates and Policy Implications," at http://www.rand.org/pubs/technical_reports/2006/RAND_TR300.pdf.

[28] CRS Report RS22945, *Flood Insurance Requirements for Stafford Act Assistance*, by Edward C. Liu.

[29] Howard C. Kunreuther, "The Changing Societal Consequences of Risks from Natural Hazards." Annals of theAmerican Academy of Political and Social Science 1979, vol. 443, p. 104-116.

[30] National Committee on Levee Safety, *Recommendations for a National Levee Safety Program. A Report to Congress from the National Committee on Levee Safety*, January 15, 2009, at http://www.iwr.usace.army.mil/ncls/docs/NCLS-Recommendation-Report_012009_DRAFT.pdf.

[31] For more information on FEMA's Map Modernization, see *FEMA Map Modernization: An Overview*, http://www.fema.gov/plan/prevent/fhm/mm_main.shtm.

[32] U.S. Department of Homeland Security, Federal Emergency Management Agency, "FEMA: Availability of Flood Hazard Maps and Data," *Federal Register*, vol. 73, no. 206, October 23, 2008, p. 63184.

[33] Ibid.

[34] 44 CFR 59.21.

[35] National Wildlife Federation, *Heavy Rainfall and Increased Flooding Risk: Global Warming's Wake-up Call for the Central United States*, 2008, at http://www.nwf.org/extremeweather/pdfs/Heavy_Rainfall_and_Increased_Flooding-Wake-Up_Call_for_Central_U.S2.pdf.

[36] U.S. Department of Homeland Security, Office of Inspector General, "FEMA Policy Related to Coastal Velocity Zones," OIG-09-71, May 27, 2009, at http://www.dhs.gov/xoig/assets/mgmtrpts/OIG_09-71_May09.pdf.

[37] U.S. President Jimmy Carter, "Floodplain Management" Executive Order 11988, *Federal Register,* May 24, 1977, p. 26951, at http://www.fema.gov/plan/ehp/ehplaws/attachments-laws/eo11988.pdf.

[38] For more information, see CRS Report RL33892, *Post-Katrina Insurance Issues Surrounding Water Damage Exclusions in Homeowners' Insurance Policies*, by Rawle O. King.

[39] Memorandum from Consumer Federation of American and other Organizations, *National Catastrophe Policy Legislation*, December 9, 2008, at http://smartnatcat.org/files/coalition_transition_memorandum.pdf.

[40] See Carolyn Kouky and Howard Kunreuther, "Improving Flood Insurance and Flood Risk Management: Insights from St. Louis, Missouri," *Resources for the Future*, February 2009, at http://www.rff.org/rff/documents/rff-dp-09-07.pdf.

[41] Dwight Jaffee and Howard Kunreuther and E. Michael-Kerja, "Long-Term Insurance for Addressing Catastrophic risk," *National Bureau of Economic Research Working Paper*, August 2008.

In: National and Mandatory Flood Insurance ISBN: 978-1-61209-126-6
Editors: A. Muñoz and M. Phillips

Chapter 2

NATIONAL FLOOD INSURANCE PROGRAM: CONTINUED ACTIONS NEEDED TO ADDRESS FINANCIAL AND OPERATIONAL ISSUES

Orice Williams Brown

WHY GAO DID THIS STUDY

The National Flood Insurance Program (NFIP), established in 1968, provides policyholders with insurance coverage for flood damage. The Federal Emergency Management Agency (FEMA) within the Department of Homeland Security is responsible for managing NFIP. Unprecedented losses from the 2005 hurricane season and NFIP's periodic need to borrow from the U.S. Treasury to pay flood insurance claims have raised concerns about the program's long-term financial solvency. Because of these concerns and NFIP's operational issues, NFIP has been on GAO's high-risk list since March 2006. As of August 2010, NFIP's debt to Treasury stood at $18.8 billion. This testimony discusses (1) NFIP's financial challenges, (2) FEMA's operational and management challenges, and (3) actions needed to address these challenges. In preparing this statement, GAO relied on its past work on NFIP and GAO's ongoing review of FEMA's management of NFIP, particularly data management and contractor oversight issues.

What GAO Recommends

In past work, GAO recommended, among other things, that FEMA take steps to help ensure that premium rates are more reflective of flood risks; strengthen its oversight of NFIP and insurance companies responsible for selling and servicing flood policies; and strengthen its internal controls and data quality. FEMA has begun to take steps to address some of these recommendations.

What GAO Found

While Congress and FEMA intended that NFIP be funded with premiums collected from policyholders rather than with tax dollars, the program is, by design, not actuarially sound. NFIP cannot do some of the things that private insurers do to manage their risks. For example, NFIP is not structured to build a capital surplus, is likely unable to purchase reinsurance to cover catastrophic losses, cannot reject high-risk applicants, and is subject to statutory limits on rate increases. In addition, its premium rates do not reflect actual flood risk. For example, nearly one in four property owners pay subsidized rates, "full-risk" rates may not reflect the full risk of flooding, and NFIP allows "grandfathered" rates that allow some property owners to continue paying rates that do not reflect reassessments of their properties' flood risk. Further, NFIP cannot deny insurance on the basis of frequent losses and thus provides policies for repetitive loss properties, which represent only 1 percent of policies but account for 25 to 30 percent of claims. NFIP's financial condition has improved slightly due to an increase in the number of policyholders and moderate flood losses, and since March 2009, FEMA has taken some encouraging steps toward improving its financial position, including making $600 million in payments to Treasury without increasing its borrowings. However, it is unlikely to pay off its full $18.8 billion debt, especially if it faces catastrophic loss years.

Operational and management issues may also limit efforts to address NFIP's financial challenges and meet program goals. Payments to write-your-own (WYO) insurers, which are key to NFIP operations, represent one-third to two-thirds of the premiums collected. But FEMA does not systematically consider actual flood insurance expense information when calculating these payments and has not aligned its WYO bonus structure with NFIP goals or implemented all of its financial controls for the WYO program. GAO also found that FEMA did not consistently follow its procedures for monitoring non-WYO contractors or coordinate contract monitoring responsibilities among departments on some contracts. Some contract monitoring records were missing, and no system was in place that would allow departments to share information on contractor deficiencies. In ongoing GAO work examining FEMA's management of NFIP, some similar issues are emerging. For example, FEMA does not have an effective system to manage flood insurance policy and claims data, although investing roughly 7 years and $40 million on a new system whose development has been halted. However, FEMA has begun to acknowledge its management challenges and develop a plan of action.

Addressing the financial challenges facing NFIP would likely require actions by both FEMA and Congress that involve trade-offs, and the challenges could be difficult to remedy. For example, reducing subsidies could increase collected premiums but reduce program participation. At the same time, FEMA must address its operational and management issues. GAO has recommended a number of actions that FEMA could take to improve NFIP operations, and ongoing work will likely identify additional issues.

Chairman Dodd, Ranking Member Shelby, and Members of the Committee:

I appreciate the opportunity to participate in today's hearing on the National Flood Insurance Program (NFIP) and the challenges that the Federal Emergency Management Agency (FEMA) faces in administering it. As you know, NFIP is a key component of the federal government's efforts to minimize the damage and financial impact of floods and is the only source of insurance against flood damage for most residents in flood-prone areas. GAO placed NFIP on its high-risk list in March 2006, not only because of the program's potential to incur billions of dollars in losses and the many financial challenges it faces, but also because of operational and management challenges within FEMA, many of which we have identified in previous reports to Congress.

As of August 2010, NFIP owed approximately $18.8 billion to the Department of the Treasury (Treasury), primarily as a result of loans the program received to pay claims from the 2005 hurricane season. NFIP borrowed additional funds from Treasury to make interest payments on this debt and is unlikely ever to be able to repay the entire amount. These revenue shortfalls reflect both the devastating effects of catastrophic hurricanes and structural weaknesses in the way the program is funded. Our previous reports identified many of these weaknesses, including subsidized premium rates, rate-setting methods that do not reflect the actual risk of losses due to flooding, and claims arising from a small, but growing number of repetitive loss properties.[1] We have also previously identified management issues, particularly with respect to FEMA's oversight of write-your-own (WYO) insurers. We are currently conducting a comprehensive review of NFIP management and other ongoing challenges that FEMA faces in administering the program as well as a review of the NFIP mapping program.

My testimony today will revisit and update the challenges we identified in previous reports, specifically (1) NFIP's financial challenges, (2) FEMA's operational and management challenges relating to NFIP, and (3) actions needed to address these challenges. My statement is based largely on completed work on the oversight of the WYO program, the financial impact of subsidized premium rates, and the rate-setting process for flood insurance premiums. We performed our work in accordance with generally accepted government auditing standards. Those standards require that we plan and perform the audit to obtain sufficient, appropriate evidence to provide a reasonable basis for our findings and conclusions based on our audit objectives. We believe that the evidence we obtained provides a reasonable basis for our findings and conclusions based on our audit objectives.

SUMMARY

Congress and FEMA intended that the NFIP's operating expenses and flood insurance claims would be paid with premiums collected by the program rather than with tax dollars. But the program is, by design, not actuarially sound, for several reasons. First, NFIP does not operate like private insurance companies. For example, FEMA is not structured to build a capital surplus, is likely unable to purchase reinsurance to cover high or catastrophic losses, cannot accept or reject applicants to help manage risk, and is subject to statutory limits on rate increases. Second, many property owners pay premium rates that do not reflect the full, long-term risk of flooding. Almost 25 percent of property owners pay subsidized premium rates, and even "full-risk" premium rates may not reflect the actual risk of flooding. Further, NFIP allows some property owners to continue to pay rates that do not reflect reassessments of their properties' flood risk ("grandfathered rates"). Finally, NFIP must continue to insure repetitive loss properties, which represent only 1 percent of flood insurance policies but account for 25 to 30 percent of claims. FEMA has taken some encouraging steps toward improving its financial position, including making nearly $600 million in payments to the U.S. Treasury since March 2009 without increasing its borrowing. In addition, according to FEMA data, as of June 2010 it has also increased its amount of collected premiums by approximately 24 percent since December 2006 and the NFIP policy base by more than 24 percent since 2004, when FEMA began its FloodSmart program.[2]

Several operational and management issues may limit FEMA's progress in addressing NFIP's financial challenges and achieving the program's goals. For example, WYO insurers play a key role in NFIP operations and payments to them represent from one-third to two-thirds of premiums received. But in previous reports we found that, among other internal control weaknesses, FEMA did not systematically consider actual flood insurance expense information when determining payments to WYO insurers, had not aligned its WYO bonus structure with NFIP's goals, and had not implemented many of its planned financial controls for the WYO program.[3] Further, contractors other than WYO insurers are responsible for performing key NFIP functions, such as collecting NFIP data and marketing the program. However, we have also found problems with oversight of these contractors. Specifically, FEMA did not consistently follow its procedures for monitoring contractors, did not always coordinate contract monitoring responsibilities among various agency departments on some of the contracts we reviewed, lacked contract monitoring records, and did not have a system in place that would allow various departments to share information relating to contractor deficiencies. Further, preliminary results of our ongoing work reveal that FEMA continues to lack an effective system to manage flood insurance policy and claims data, despite having invested roughly 7 years and $40 million in a new system whose development has been halted because it did not meet user needs and was not ready to replace the legacy system.

Addressing the financial and operational challenges facing NFIP would require actions from both Congress and FEMA. We recognize that any such actions would involve significant trade-offs and that some financial challenges would be difficult to remedy. For instance, possible reform options to make premium rates more reflective of long-term flood risks include eliminating, reducing, or targeting premium subsidies based on need. But taking any of these steps would raise rates and potentially reduce participation in NFIP. FEMA and Congress could also address the impact of repetitive loss properties by expanding mitigation efforts to target those properties that are at highest risk.[4] However, doing so would include actions such as elevation, relocation, and demolition that would be costly to taxpayers and could take years. Congress could also amend laws regarding coverage for homeowners who refuse to mitigate, and streamline the various mitigation grant programs within FEMA. In our past work, we also identified a number of management challenges that FEMA would have to address, including improvements to oversight of WYO insurers and its payments to them, updating the NFIP rate-setting process, fully applying internal controls, and strengthening oversight of contractors, among others.

BACKGROUND

The National Flood Insurance Act of 1968 established NFIP as an alternative to providing direct assistance after floods.[5] NFIP, which provides government-guaranteed flood insurance to homeowners and businesses, was intended to reduce the federal government's escalating costs for repairing flood damage after disasters. FEMA, which is within the Department of Homeland Security (DHS), is responsible for the oversight and management of NFIP. Since NFIP's inception, Congress has enacted several pieces of legislation to strengthen the program. The Flood Disaster Protection Act of 1973 made flood insurance mandatory for owners of properties in vulnerable areas who had mortgages from federally regulated lenders and provided additional incentives for communities to join the program.[6] The National Flood Insurance Reform Act of 1994 strengthened the mandatory purchase requirements for owners of properties located in special flood hazard areas (SFHA) with mortgages from federally regulated lenders.[7] Finally, the Bunning-Bereuter-Blumenauer Flood Insurance Reform Act of 2004 authorized grant programs to mitigate properties that experienced repetitive flooding losses. Owners of these repetitive loss properties who do not mitigate face higher premiums.[8]

To participate in NFIP, communities agree to enforce regulations for land use and new construction in high-risk flood zones and to adopt and enforce state and community floodplain management regulations to reduce future flood damage. Currently, more than 20,000 communities participate in NFIP. NFIP has mapped flood risks across the country, assigning flood zone designations based on risk levels, and these designations are a factor in determining premium rates. NFIP offers two types of flood insurance premiums: subsidized and full-risk. The National Flood Insurance Act of 1968 authorizes NFIP to offer subsidized premiums to owners of certain properties. These subsidized premium rates, which represent about 35 to 40 percent of the cost of covering the full risk of flood damage to the properties, account for about 22 percent of all NFIP policies as of September 2010. To help reduce or eliminate the long-term risk of flood damage to buildings and other structures insured by NFIP, FEMA has used a variety of mitigation efforts such as elevation, relocation, and demolition. Despite these efforts, the inventories of repetitive loss properties and policies with subsidized premium rates have continued to grow. In response to the magnitude and severity of the losses from the 2005 hurricanes, Congress increased NFIP's borrowing authority from the Treasury to $20.775 billion. As of August 2010, FEMA owed Treasury $18.8 billion, and the program as currently designed will likely not generate sufficient revenues to repay this debt.

NFIP's Financial Challenges Have Increased the Federal Government's and U.S. Taxpayers' Financial Exposure from Flood Losses

By design, NFIP is not an actuarially sound program, in part because it does not operate like many private insurance companies. As a government program, its primary public policy goal is to provide flood insurance in flood-prone areas to property owners who otherwise would not be able to obtain it. Yet NFIP is also expected to cover its claims losses and operating expenses with the premiums it collects, much like a private insurer. In years when flooding has not been catastrophic, NFIP has generally managed to meet these competing goals. In years of catastrophic flooding, however, and especially during the 2005 hurricane season, it has not.

NFIP's operations differ from those of most private insurers in a number of ways. First, it operates on a cash-flow basis and has the authority to borrow from Treasury. As of August 2010, NFIP owed approximately $18.8 billion to Treasury, primarily as a result of loans that the program received to pay claims from the 2005 hurricane season. NFIP will likely not be able to meet its interest payments in most years, and the debt may continue to grow as the program may need to borrow to meet the interest payments in some years and potential future flood losses. Also unlike private insurance companies, NFIP assumes all the risk for the policies it sells. Private insurers typically retain only part of the risk that they accept from policyholders, ceding a portion of the risk to reinsurers (insurance for insurers). This mechanism is particularly important in the case of insurance for catastrophic events, because the availability of reinsurance allows an insurer to limit the possibility that it will experience losses beyond its ability to pay. NFIP's lack of reinsurance, combined with the lack of structure to build a capital surplus, transfers much of the financial risk of flooding to Treasury and ultimately the taxpayer.

NFIP is also required to accept virtually all applications for insurance, unlike private insurers, which may reject applicants for a variety of reasons. For example, FEMA cannot deny insurance on the basis of frequent losses. As a result, NFIP is less able to offset the effects of adverse selection—that is, the phenomenon that those who are most likely to purchase insurance are also the most likely to experience losses. Adverse selection may lead to a concentration of policyholders in the riskiest areas. This problem is further compounded by the fact that those at greatest risk are required to purchase insurance from NFIP if they have a mortgage from a federally regulated lender. Finally, by law, FEMA is prevented from raising rates on each flood zone by more than 10 percent each year. While most states regulate premium prices for private insurance companies on other lines of insurance, they generally do not set limits on premium rate increases, instead focusing on whether the resulting premium rates are justified by the projected losses and expenses.

NFIP's Premium Rates Do Not Reflect the Full Risk of Flooding

As we have seen, NFIP does not charge rates that reflect the full risk of flooding. NFIP could be placed on a sounder fiscal footing by addressing several elements of its premium structure. For example, as we have pointed out in previous reports, NFIP provides subsidized and grandfathered rates that do not reflect the full risk of potential flood losses to some property owners, operates in part with unreliable and incomplete data on flood risks that make it difficult to set accurate rates, and has not been able to overcome the challenge of repetitive loss properties.[9] Subsidized rates, which are required by law, are perhaps the best-known example of premium rates that do not reflect the actual risk of flooding. These rates, which were authorized from when the program began, were intended to help property owners during the transition to full-risk rates. But today, nearly one out of four NFIP policies continues to be based on a subsidized rate. These rates allow policyholders with structures that were built before floodplain management regulations were established in their communities to pay premiums that represent about 35 to 40 percent of the actual risk premium. Moreover, FEMA estimates that properties covered by policies with subsidized rates experience as much as five times more flood damage than compliant new structures that are charged full-risk rates. As we have pointed out, the number of policies receiving subsidized rates has grown steadily in recent years and without changes to the program will likely continue to grow, increasing the potential for future NFIP operating deficits.

Further, potentially outdated and inaccurate data about flood probabilities and damage claims, as well as outdated flood maps, raise questions about whether full-risk premiums fully reflect the actual risk of flooding. First, some of the data used to estimate the probability of flooding have not been updated since the 1980s. Similarly, the claims data used as inputs to the model may be inaccurate because of incomplete claims records and missing data. Further, some of the maps FEMA uses to set premium rates remain out of date despite recent modernization efforts. For instance, as FEMA continues these modernization efforts, it does not account for ongoing and planned development making some maps outdated shortly after their completion. Moreover, FEMA does not map for long-term erosion, further increasing the likelihood that data used to set rates are inaccurate. FEMA also sets flood insurance rates on a nationwide basis, failing to account for many topographic factors that are relevant to flood risk for individual properties. Some patterns in historical claims and premium data suggest that NFIP's rates may not accurately reflect individual differences in properties' flood risk. Not accurately reflecting the actual risk of flooding increases the risk that full-risk premiums may not be sufficient to cover future losses and add to concerns about NFIP's financial stability.

As mentioned earlier, we are currently reviewing FEMA's flood mapping program. Specifically, we are trying to determine the extent to which FEMA ensures that flood maps accurately reflect flood risk and the methods FEMA uses to promote community acceptance of flood maps. We plan to issue this chapter in December 2010.[10]

Further contributing to NFIP's financial challenges, FEMA made a policy decision to allow certain properties remapped into riskier flood zones to keep their previous lower rates. Like subsidized rates, these "grandfathered" rates do not reflect the actual risk of flooding to the properties and do not generate sufficient premiums to cover expected losses. FEMA officials told us that the decision to grandfather rates was based on considerations of equity, ease of administration, and goals of promoting floodplain management. However,

FEMA does not collect data on grandfathered properties or measure their financial impact on the program. As a result, it does not know how many such properties exist, their exact location, or the volume of losses they generate. FEMA officials stated that beginning in October 2010 they would indicate on all new policies whether or not they were grandfathered. However, they would still be unable to identify grandfathered properties among existing policies. As FEMA continues its efforts to modernize flood maps across the country, it has continued to face resistance from communities and homeowners when remapping properties into higher-risk flood zones with higher rates. As a result, FEMA has often grandfathered in previous premium rates that are lower than the remapped rates. However, homeowners who are remapped into high-risk areas and do not currently have flood insurance may be required to purchase it at the full risk rate.

In reauthorizing NFIP in 2004, Congress noted that repetitive loss properties—those that have had two or more flood insurance claims payments of $1,000 or more over 10 years—constituted a significant drain on NFIP resources. These properties account for about 1 percent of all policies but are estimated to account for up to 30 percent of all NFIP losses. Not all repetitive loss properties are part of the subsidized property inventory, but a high proportion receive subsidized rates, further contributing to NFIP's financial risks. While Congress has made efforts to target these properties, the number of repetitive loss properties has continued to grow, making them an ongoing challenge to NFIP's financial stability.

Despite Its Financial Challenges, NFIP Has Experienced Some Positive Developments

According to FEMA, expanded marketing efforts through its FloodSmart campaign have contributed to an increase in NFIP policies. This program was designed to educate and inform partners, stakeholders, property owners, and renters about insuring their homes and businesses against flood damage. Since the start of the FloodSmart campaign in 2004, NFIP has seen policy growth of more than 24 percent, and as of June 2010, had 5.6 million policies in force. Moreover, according to FEMA, despite the economic downturn, both policy sales and retention have grown. In addition, NFIP's collected premiums have risen 24 percent from December 2006 to June 2010. This increase, combined with a relatively low loss experience in recent years, has enabled FEMA to make nearly $600 million in payments to Treasury with no additional borrowing since March 2009. FEMA has also adjusted its expense reimbursement formula. While these are all encouraging developments, FEMA is still unlikely to ever pay off its current $18.8 billion debt.

FEMA's Operational and Management Issues May Further Limit Progress in Achieving NFIP Goals

We have identified a number of operational issues that affect NFIP, including weaknesses in FEMA's oversight of WYO insurers, and shortcomings in its oversight of other contractors, as well as new issues from ongoing work. For example, we found that FEMA does not systematically consider actual flood insurance expense information when determining the amount it pays WYO insurers for selling and servicing flood insurance policies and adjusting claims. Instead, FEMA has used proxies, such as average industry operating expenses for property insurance, to determine the rates at which it pays these insurers, even though their actual flood insurance expense information has been available since 1997. Because FEMA does not systematically consider these data when setting its payment rates, it cannot effectively estimate how much insurers are spending to carry out their contractual obligations to FEMA. Further, FEMA does not compare the WYO insurers' actual expenses to the payments they receive each year and thus cannot determine whether the payments are reasonable in terms of expenses and profits. When GAO compared payments FEMA made to six WYO insurers to their actual expenses for calendar years 2005 through 2007, we found that the payments exceeded actual expenses by $327.1 million, or 16.5 percent of total payments made. By considering actual expense information, FEMA could provide greater transparency and accountability over payments to the WYO insurers and potentially save taxpayers' funds.

FEMA also has not aligned its bonus structure for WYO insurers with NFIP goals such as increasing penetration in low-risk flood zones and among homeowners in all zones that do not have mortgages from federally regulated lenders. FEMA uses a broad-based distribution formula that primarily rewards companies that are new to NFIP, and can relatively easily increase their percentage of net policies from a small base. We also found that most WYO insurers generally offered flood insurance when it was requested but did not strategically market the product as a primary insurance line. FEMA has set only one explicit marketing goal—to increase policy growth by 5 percent each year—and does not review the WYO insurers' marketing plans. It therefore lacks the information needed to assess the effectiveness of either the WYO insurers' efforts to increase participation or the bonus program itself. For example, FEMA does not know the extent to which sales increases may reflect external factors such as flood events or its own FloodSmart marketing campaign rather than any effort on the part of the insurers. Having intermediate targeted goals could also help expand program participation, and linking such goals directly to the bonus structure could help ensure that NFIP and WYO goals are in line with each other.

Finally, FEMA has explicit financial control requirements and procedures for the WYO program but has not implemented all aspects of its Financial Control Plan. FEMA's Financial Control Plan provides guidance for WYO insurers to help ensure compliance with the statutory requirements for NFIP. It contains several checks and balances to help ensure that taxpayers' funds are spent appropriately. For an earlier report, we reviewed 10 WYO insurers and found that while FEMA performed most of the required biennial audits and underwriting and claims reviews required under the plan, it rarely or never implemented most of the required audits for cause, reviews of state insurance department audits, or marketing, litigation, and customer service operational reviews.[11] In addition, FEMA did not systematically track the outcomes of the various audits, inspections, and reviews that it performed. We also found that multiple units had responsibility for helping ensure that WYO insurers complied with each component of the Financial Control Plan; that FEMA did not maintain a single, comprehensive monitoring system that would allow it to ensure compliance with all components of the plan; and that there was no centralized access to all of the documentation produced. Because FEMA does not implement all aspects of the Financial Control Plan, it cannot ensure that WYOs are fully complying with program requirements.

In another review, we found that weak internal controls impaired FEMA's ability to maintain effective transaction-level accountability with WYO insurers from fiscal years 2005 through 2007, a period that included the financial activity related to the 2005 Gulf Coast hurricanes.[12] NFIP had limited assurance that its financial data for fiscal years 2005 to 2007 were accurate. This impaired data reliability resulted from weaknesses at all three levels of the NFIP transaction accountability and financial reporting process. At the WYO level, WYO insurer claims loss files did not include the documents necessary to support the claims, and some companies filed reports late, undermining the reliability of the data they did report. Second, contractor-level internal control activities were ineffective in verifying the accuracy of the data that WYO insurers submitted, such as names and addresses. Lastly, at the agency level, financial reporting process controls were not based on transaction-level data. Instead FEMA relied primarily on summary data compiled using error-prone manual data entry.

FEMA's Oversight of Non-WYO Contractor Activities Is also Lacking

Also in a previous report, we pointed out that FEMA lacked records of monitoring activities for other contractors, inconsistently followed its procedures for monitoring these contractors, and did not coordinate contract monitoring responsibilities for the two major contracts we reviewed.[13] At FEMA, a Contracting Officer's Technical Representative (COTR) and staff (referred to as "monitors") are responsible for, respectively, ensuring compliance with contract terms and regularly monitoring and reporting on the extent to which NFIP contractors meet standards in performance areas specified in the contracts. Internal control standards for the federal government state that records should be properly managed and maintained. But FEMA lacked records for the majority of the monitoring reports we requested and did not consistently follow the monitoring procedures for preparing, reviewing, and maintaining monitoring reports.

Further, FEMA offices did not coordinate information and actions relating to contractors' deficiencies and payments, and in some cases key officials were unaware of decisions on contractors' performance. In particular, our review of monitoring reports for one contract revealed a lack of coordination between the COTR and the contracting officer. As a result, FEMA could not ensure that the contractor had adhered to the contract's requirements and lacked information critical to effective oversight of key NFIP data collection, reporting, and insurance functions. Given NFIP's reliance on contractors, it is important that FEMA have in place adequate controls that are consistently applied to all contracts. Consistent with our findings in prior work, the DHS inspector general has also identified weaknesses in FEMA's internal controls and financial reporting related to the NFIP.[14]

Our ongoing work reviewing FEMA's management of NFIP identifies a number of steps that FEMA has taken that are designed to improve the agency's oversight of contractors. These efforts include the implementation of an acquisition review board and the creation of a handbook for COTRs. While these are positives steps, not enough time has passed to evaluate their effectiveness.

FEMA Continues to Lack an Effective System to Manage Flood Insurance Policy and Claims Data

To manage the flood policy and claims information that it obtains from insurance companies, NFIP's Bureau and Statistical Agent (BSA) relies on a flood insurance management system from the 1980s that is difficult and costly to sustain and that does not adequately support NFIP's mission needs. This system consists of over 70 interfaced applications that utilize monthly tape and batch submissions of policy and claims data from insurance companies. The system also provides limited access to NFIP data. Further, identifying and correcting errors in submission requires between 30 days and 6 months and the general claims processing cycle itself is 2 to 3 months.

To address the limitations of this system, NFIP launched a program in 2002 to acquire and implement a modernization and business improvement system, known as NextGen. As envisioned, NextGen was to accelerate updates to information obtained from insurance companies, identify errors before flood insurance policies went into effect, and enable FEMA to expedite business transactions and responses to NFIP claims when policyholders required urgent support. As such, the system would support the needs of a wide range of NFIP stakeholders, including FEMA headquarters and regional staff, WYO insurers, vendors, state hazard mitigation officers, and NFIP state coordinators.

As part of our ongoing review of FEMA's management of NFIP, we found that despite having invested roughly $40 million over 7 years, FEMA has yet to implement NextGen. Initial versions of NextGen were first deployed for operational use in May 2008. However, shortly thereafter system users reported major problems with the system, including significant data and processing errors. As a result, use of NextGen was halted, and the agency returned to relying exclusively on its mainframe-based legacy system while NextGen underwent additional testing. In late 2009, after this testing showed that the system did not meet user needs and was not ready to replace the legacy system, further development and deployment of NextGen was stopped, and FEMA's Chief Information Officer began an evaluation to determine what, if anything, associated with the system could be salvaged. This evaluation is currently under way, and a date for completing it has yet to be established. DHS and the Office of Management and Budget recently designated this effort as high-risk.

Our ongoing review of FEMA's management of NFIP includes identifying lessons learned about how NextGen was defined, developed, tested, and deployed, including weaknesses in requirements development and management, test management, risk management, executive oversight, and program office staffing that have collectively contributed to NextGen's failure. In completing its evaluation and deciding how to proceed in meeting its policy and claims processing needs, FEMA could benefit by correcting these weaknesses. In the interim, the agency continues to rely on its outdated legacy system, and thus does not have the kind of robust analytical support and information needed to help address the reasons that NFIP remains on GAO's high-risk list of federal programs.

ADDRESSING NFIP'S CHALLENGES WOULD REQUIRE ACTIONS FROM FEMA AND CONGRESS

To address the challenges NFIP faces, FEMA would have to address its own operational and management challenges. Further, legislative reform would be needed to address structural issues. However, as you know, addressing many of these issues involves public policy trade-offs that would have to be made by Congress. In July 2010 the House of Representatives passed the Flood Insurance Reform Priorities Act, which if enacted would make a number of changes to NFIP.[15] Moreover, part of this process requires determining whether NFIP is or should be structured as an insurance program and how much liability the government can and is willing to accept. For example, if Congress wants to structure NFIP as an insurance company and limit borrowing from Treasury in future high- or catastrophic loss years, NFIP would have to build a capital surplus fund. Our prior work has shown that building such a fund would require charging premium rates that, in some cases, could be more than double or triple current rates and would take a number of years without catastrophic losses to implement. Additionally, while private insurers generally use reinsurance to hedge their risk of catastrophic losses, it is unclear whether the private reinsurance market would be willing to offer coverage to NFIP. In the absence of reinsurance and a surplus fund, Treasury will effectively continue to act as the reinsurer for NFIP and be the financial backstop for the program.

Premium Rates Could Be Made More Reflective of Flood Risk

Making premium rates more reflective of flood risk would require actions by FEMA and Congress. Because subsidized premium rates are required by law, addressing their associated costs would require congressional action. As previously reported, two potential options would be to eliminate or reduce the use of subsidies over time, or target them based on need. However, these options involve trade-offs. For example, eliminating or reducing the subsidies would help ensure that premium rates more accurately reflect the actual risk of loss and could encourage mitigation efforts. But the resulting higher premiums could lead some homeowners to discontinue or not purchase coverage, thus reducing participation in NFIP and potentially increasing the costs to taxpayers of providing disaster assistance in the event of a catastrophe. Targeting subsidies based on need is an approach used by other federal programs and could help ensure that those needing the subsidy would have access to it and retain their coverage. Unlike other agencies that provide—and are allocated funds for—traditional subsidies, NFIP does not receive an appropriation to pay for shortfalls in collected premiums caused by its subsidized rates.

However, one option to maintain the subsidies but improve NFIP's financial stability would be to rate all policies at the full-risk rate and to appropriate subsidies for qualified policyholders. In this way, the cost of such subsidies would be more transparent, and policyholders would be better informed of their flood risk. Depending on how such a program was implemented, NFIP might be able to charge more participants rates that more accurately reflect their risk of flooding. However, raising premium rates for some participants could also decrease program participation, and low-income property owners and renters could be discouraged from participating in NFIP if they were required to prove that they met the requirements for a subsidy. FEMA might also face challenges in implementing this option in the midst of other ongoing operational and management challenges.

NFIP's rate-setting process for full-risk premiums may not ensure that those premium rates reflect the actual risk of flooding and therefore may increase NFIP's financial risk. Moreover, FEMA's rate-setting process for subsidized properties depends, in part, on the accuracy of the full-risk rates, raising concerns about how subsidized rates are calculated as well. To address these concerns, we have identified actions that FEMA could take. For example, we recommended that FEMA take steps to help ensure that its rate-setting methods and the data it uses to set rates result in full-risk premium rates that accurately reflect the risk of losses from flooding. In particular, we pointed out that these steps should include verifying the accuracy of flood probabilities, damage estimates, and flood maps, and reevaluating the practice of aggregating risks across zones.

Similarly, because NFIP allows grandfathered rates for those remapped into high-risk flood zones, it would also be in the position to address some of the challenges associated with this practice. FEMA could end grandfathered rates, but it decided to allow grandfathering after consulting with Congress, its oversight committees, and other stakeholders and considering issues of equity, fairness, and the goal of promoting floodplain management. We recommended that the agency take steps both to ensure that information was collected on the location, number, and losses associated with existing and newly created grandfathered properties in NFIP and to analyze the financial impact of these properties on the flood insurance program.[16] With such information, FEMA and Congress will be better informed on the extent to which these rates contribute to NFIP's financial challenges.

Another statutory requirement that could be revisited is the 10-percent cap on rate increases. As with all the potential reform options, determining whether such action is warranted would necessitate weighing the law's benefits—including limiting financial hardship to policyholders—against the benefits that increasing or removing such limits would provide to NFIP, Treasury, and ultimately the taxpayer. However, as long as caps on rate increases remain, FEMA will continue to face financial challenges.

Solutions for addressing the impact of repetitive loss properties would also require action by both FEMA and Congress. For example, we have reported that one option for Congress would be to substantially expand mitigation efforts and target these efforts toward the highest-risk properties.[17] Mitigation criteria could be made more stringent – for example, by requiring all insured properties that have filed two or more flood claims (even for small amounts) to mitigate, denying insurance to property owners who refuse or do not respond to a mitigation offer, or some combination of these approaches. While these actions would help reduce losses from flood damage and could ultimately limit costs to taxpayers by decreasing the number of subsidized properties, they would require increased funding for FEMA's mitigation programs, to elevate, relocate, or demolish the properties, would be costly to taxpayers, and could take years to complete. Congress could also consider changes to address loopholes in mitigation and repurchase requirements that allow policyholders to avoid mitigating by simply not responding to FEMA's requests that they do so. FEMA could be required to either drop coverage for such properties or use eminent domain to seize them if owners fail to respond to FEMA's mitigation requests. Moreover, Congress could streamline the various mitigation grant programs to make them more efficient and effective.[18]

FEMA Could Take Further Actions to Help Address Operational and Management Challenges

Over the last several years we have made many recommendations for actions that FEMA could take to improve its management of NFIP. FEMA has implemented some recommendations, including among other things, introducing a statistically valid method for sampling flood insurance claims for review, establishing a regulatory appeals process for policyholders, and ensuring that WYO insurance agents meet minimum education and training requirements.[19] FEMA has also taken steps to make analyzing the overall results of claims adjustments easier after future flood events. The efforts will help in determining the number and type of claims adjustment errors made and deciding whether new, cost-efficient methods for adjusting claims that were introduced after Hurricane Katrina are feasible to use after other flood events.[20] However, as mentioned previously, many of our other previous recommendations have not yet been implemented. For example, we have recommended that FEMA:

- Address challenges to oversight of the WYO program, specifically the lack of transparency of and accountability for the payments FEMA makes to WYO insurers, by determining in advance the amounts built into the payment rates for estimated expenses and profit, annually analyzing the amounts of actual expenses and profit in relation to the estimated amounts used in setting payment rates, and by immediately reassessing the practice of paying WYO insurers an additional 1 percent of written premiums for operating expenses.
- Take steps to better oversee WYO insurers and ensure that they are in compliance with statutory requirements for NFIP and that taxpayers' funds are spent appropriately by consistently following the Financial Control Plan and ensuring that each component is implemented; ensuring that any revised Financial Control Plan covers oversight of all functions of participating WYO insurers, including customer service and litigation expenses; systematically tracking insurance companies' compliance with and performance under each component of the Financial Control Plan; and ensuring centralized access to all

audits, reviews, and data analyses performed for each WYO insurer under the Financial Control Plan.

- Improve NFIP's transaction-level accountability and assure that financial reporting is accurate and that insurance company operations conform to program requirements by augmenting NFIP policies to require contractors to develop procedures for analyzing financial reports in relation to the transaction-level information that WYO insurers submit for statistical purposes; revising required internal control activities for contractors to provide for verifying and validating the reliability of WYO-reported financial information based on a review of a sample of the underlying transactions or events; and obtaining verification that these objectives have been met through independent audits of the WYO insurers.
- Address contract and management oversight issues that we have identified in previous reports, including determining the feasibility of integrating and streamlining numerous existing NFIP financial reporting processes to reduce the risk of errors inherent in the manual recording of accounting transactions into multiple systems; establishing and implementing procedures that require the review of available information, such as the results of biennial audits, operational reviews, and claim reinspections to determine whether the targeted audits for cause should be used; establishing and implementing procedures to schedule and conduct all required operational reviews within the prescribed 3-year period; and establishing and implementing procedures to select statistically representative samples of all claims as a basis for conducting reinspections of claims by general adjusters.
- Address challenges to oversight of contractor activities, including implementing processes to ensure that monitoring reports are submitted on time and systematically reviewed and maintained by the COTR and the Program Management Office; ensuring that staff clearly monitor each performance standard the contractor is required to meet in the specified time frames and clearly link monitoring reports and performance areas; implementing written guidance for all NFIP-related contracts on how to consistently handle the failure of a contractor to meet performance standards; establishing written policies and procedures governing coordination among FEMA officials and offices when addressing contractor deficiencies; and

ensuring that financial disincentives are appropriately and consistently applied.

Building on our prior work and these recommendations, we are in the process of conducting a comprehensive review of FEMA's overall management of NFIP that could help FEMA develop a roadmap for identifying and addressing many of the root causes of its operational and management challenges. This review focuses on a wide range of internal management issues including acquisition, contractor oversight, information technology (NextGen), internal controls, human capital, budget and resources, document management, and financial management. While our work is ongoing, we have observed some positive developments in the agency's willingness to begin to acknowledge its management issues and the need to address them. FEMA has also taken steps to improve our access to key NFIP staff and information by providing us with an on-site office at one of FEMA's locations, facilitating our ability to access and review documents. In addition, in April 2010 FEMA staff initiated a meeting with GAO to discuss all outstanding recommendations related to NFIP and the actions they planned to take to address them. We are in the process of obtaining and evaluating documentation related to these actions.

Recent Proposals Could Provide Some Benefits but also Raise Concerns

As part of our past work, we have also evaluated other proposals related to NFIP. Each of those proposals has potential benefits as well as challenges.

- In a previous report, we discussed some of the challenges associated with implementing a combined federal flood and wind insurance program.[21] While such a program could provide coverage for wind damage to those unable to obtain it in the private market and simplify the claims process for some property owners, it could also pose several challenges. For example, FEMA would need to determine wind hazard prevention standards; adapt existing programs to accommodate wind coverage, create a new rate-setting process, raise awareness of the program, enforce new building codes, and put staff and procedures in place. FEMA would also need to determine how to pay claims in years with catastrophic losses, develop a plan to respond to potential limited participation and adverse selection, and address other trade-offs, including the potential for delays in reimbursing participants, litigation, lapses in coverage, underinsured policy-holders, and larger-than-expected losses.

- As we have previously reported, private business interruption coverage for flood damage is expensive and is generally purchased only by large companies.[22] Adding business interruption insurance to NFIP could help small businesses obtain coverage that they could not obtain in the private market, but NFIP currently lacks resources and expertise in this area. Adding business interruption insurance could increase NFIP's existing debt and potentially amplify its ongoing management and financial challenges. Insurers told us that underwriting this type of coverage, properly pricing the risk, and adjusting claims was complex.
- Finally, we have reported that creating a catastrophic loss fund to pay larger-than-average annual losses would be challenging for several reasons.[23] For example, NFIP's debt to Treasury would likely prevent NFIP from ever being able to contribute to such a fund. Further, such a fund might not eliminate NFIP's need to borrow for larger-than-expected losses that occurred before the fund was fully financed. Building a fund could also require significant premium rate increases, potentially reducing participation in NFIP.

CLOSING COMMENTS

FEMA faces a number of ongoing challenges in managing and administering NFIP that, if not addressed, will continue to work against improving the program's long-term financial condition. As you know, improving NFIP's financial condition involves a set of highly complex, interrelated issues that are likely to involve many trade-offs and have no easy solutions, particularly when the solutions to problems involve balancing the goals of charging rates that reflect the full risk of flooding and encouraging broad participation in the program. In addition, addressing NFIP's current challenges will require the cooperation and participation of many stakeholders.

As we noted when placing NFIP on the high-risk list in 2006, comprehensive reform will likely be needed to address the financial challenges facing the program. In addressing these financial challenges, FEMA will also need to address a number of operational and management challenges before NFIP can be eligible for removal from the high-risk list. Our previous work has identified many of the necessary actions that FEMA should take, and preliminary observations from our ongoing work have revealed additional operational and management issues. By addressing both the financial challenges as well as the operational and management issues, NFIP will be in a much stronger position to achieve its goals and ultimately to reduce its burden on the taxpayer.

Chairman Dodd and Ranking Member Shelby, this concludes my prepared statement. I would be pleased to respond to any of the questions you or other members of the Committee may have at this time.

RELATED GAO PRODUCTS

National Flood Insurance Program: Continued Actions Needed to Address Financial and Operational Issues. GAO-10-631T. Washington, D.C.: April 21, 2010.

Financial Management: Improvements Needed in National Flood Insurance Program's Financial Controls and Oversight. GAO-10-66. Washington, D.C.: December 22, 2009.

Flood Insurance: Opportunities Exist to Improve Oversight of the WYO Program. GAO-09-455. Washington, D.C.: August 21, 2009.

Results-Oriented Management: Strengthening Key Practices at FEMA and Interior Could Promote Greater Use of Performance Information. GAO-09-676. Washington, D.C.: August 17, 2009.

Information on Proposed Changes to the National Flood Insurance Program. GAO-09-420R. Washington, D.C.: February 27, 2009.

High-Risk Series: An Update. GAO-09-271. Washington, D.C.: January 2009.

Flood Insurance: Options for Addressing the Financial Impact of Subsidized Premium Rates on the National Flood Insurance Program. GAO-09-20. Washington, D.C.: November 14, 2008.

Flood Insurance: FEMA's Rate-Setting Process Warrants Attention. GAO-09-12. Washington, D.C.: October 31, 2008.

National Flood Insurance Program: Financial Challenges Underscore Need for Improved Oversight of Mitigation Programs and Key Contracts. GAO-08-437. Washington, D.C.: June 16, 2008.

Natural Catastrophe Insurance: Analysis of a Proposed Combined Federal Flood and Wind Insurance Program. GAO-08-504. Washington, D.C.: April 25, 2008.

National Flood Insurance Program: Greater Transparency and Oversight of Wind and Flood Damage Determinations Are Needed. GAO-08-28. Washington, D.C.: December 28, 2007.

National Disasters: Public Policy Options for Changing the Federal Role in Natural Catastrophe Insurance. GAO-08-7. Washington, D.C.: November 26, 2007.

Federal Emergency Management Agency: Ongoing Challenges Facing the National Flood Insurance Program. GAO-08-118T. Washington, D.C.: October 2, 2007.

National Flood Insurance Program: FEMA's Management and Oversight of Payments for Insurance Company Services Should Be Improved. GAO-07-1078. Washington, D.C.: September 5, 2007.

National Flood Insurance Program: Preliminary Views on FEMA's Ability to Ensure Accurate Payments on Hurricane-Damaged Properties. GAO-07-991T. Washington, D.C.: June 12, 2007.

Coastal Barrier Resources System: Status of Development That Has Occurred and Financial Assistance Provided by Federal Agencies. GAO-07-356. Washington, D.C.: March 19, 2007.

National Flood Insurance Program: New Processes Aided Hurricane Katrina Claims Handling, but FEMA's Oversight Should Be Improved. GAO-07-169. Washington, D.C.: December 15, 2006.

Federal Emergency Management Agency: Challenges for the National Flood Insurance Program. GAO-06-335T. Washington, D.C.: January 25, 2006.

Federal Emergency Management Agency: Improvements Needed to Enhance Oversight and Management of the National Flood Insurance Program. GAO-06-119. Washington, D.C.: October 18, 2005.

Determining Performance and Accountability Challenges and High Risks. GAO-01-159SP. Washington, D.C.: November 2000.

End Notes

[1] Repetitive loss properties are properties that have had two or more paid NFIP claims in a 10-year period.

[2] FloodSmart is an integrated mass marketing campaign FEMA launched in 2004 to educate the public about the risks of flooding and to encourage the purchase of flood insurance.

[3] See GAO, *Flood Insurance: Opportunities Exist to Improve Oversight of the WYO Program*, GAO-09-455 (Washington, D.C.: Aug. 21, 2009).

[4] Mitigation involves taking steps to reduce a property's flood risk—for example, elevating a house above a certain flood level.

[5] Pub. L. No. 90-448, Title XIII, 82 Stat. 476 (1968).

[6] Pub. L. No. 93-234, §102, 87 Stat. 975, 978 (1973).

[7] Pub. L. No. 103-325, 108 Stat. 2255 (1994).

[8] Pub. L. No. 108-264, §§ 102, 104, 118 Stat. 712, 714, 722 (2004).

[9] See GAO, *Flood Insurance: FEMA's Rate-Setting Process Warrants Attention*, GAO-09-12 (Washington, D.C.: Oct. 31, 2008); and *Flood Insurance: Options for Addressing the Financial Impact of Subsidized Premium Rates on the National Flood Insurance Program*, GAO-09-20 (Washington, D.C.: Nov. 14, 2008).

[10] This work is being done at the request of the Chairman of the Subcommittee on Economic Policy, Senator Sherrod Brown, and Senators Charles E. Schumer and Jeff Bingaman.

[11] See GAO-09-455.

[12] See GAO, *Financial Management: Improvements Needed in National Flood Insurance Program's Financial Controls and Oversight*, GAO-10-66 (Washington, D.C.: Dec. 22, 2009).

[13] See GAO, *National Flood Insurance Program: Financial Challenges Underscore Need for Improved Oversight of Mitigation Programs and Key Contracts*, GAO-08-437 (Washington, D.C.: Jun. 16, 2008).

[14] See Department of Homeland Security, Office of the Inspector General, *Independent Auditor's Report on DHS' FY 2009 Financial Statements and Internal Control over Financial Reporting*, DHS-OIG-10-11 (Washington, D.C.: Nov. 13, 2009).

[15] H.R. 5114, Flood Insurance Reform Priorities Act of 2010, 111th Cong., 2nd Sess.

[16] See GAO-09-12.

[17] See GAO-09-20.

[18] FEMA has five different mitigation grant programs, each with different types of requirements, purposes, and appropriations: Flood Mitigation Assistance (FMA), Repetitive Flood Claims (RFC), Severe Repetitive Loss Pilot Program (SRL), Hazard Mitigation Grant Program (HMGP), and Pre-Disaster Mitigation (PDM).

[19] See GAO, *Federal Emergency Management Agency: Improvements Needed to Enhance Oversight and Management of the National Flood Insurance Program*, GAO-06-119 (Washington, D.C.: Oct. 18, 2005).

[20] See GAO, *National Flood Insurance Program: New Processes Aided Hurricane Katrina Claims Handling, but FEMA's Oversight Should Be Improved*, GAO-07-169 (Washington, D.C.: Dec. 15, 2006).

[21] See GAO, *Natural Catastrophe Insurance: Analysis of a Proposed Combined Federal Flood and Wind Insurance Program*, GAO-08-504 (Washington, D.C.: Apr. 25, 2008).

[22] See GAO, *Information on Proposed Changes to the National Flood Insurance Program*, GAO-09-420R (Washington, D.C.: Feb. 27, 2009).

[23] See GAO-09-420R.

In: National and Mandatory Flood Insurance ISBN: 978-1-61209-126-6
Editors: A. Muñoz and M. Phillips

Chapter 3

MANDATORY FLOOD INSURANCE PURCHASE IN REMAPPED RESIDUAL RISK AREAS BEHIND LEVEES

Rawle O. King

SUMMARY

This chapter examines the amount of flood insurance that must be purchased (and retained) on loans secured by real property located in federally designated special flood hazard areas (SFHAs). It is written in response to three situations: (1) the Federal Emergency Management Agency's remapping efforts that include verifying the status of all levees as providing protection against a 100-year flood, which are currently depicted on Flood Insurance Rate Maps, and widespread concerns among homeowners about new requirements to purchase flood insurance should the levee become decertified; (2) uncertainty as to whether the mandatory amount of flood insurance should be equal to the assessed value of the insured residential structure or the unpaid principal balance (UPB) of the mortgage loan; and (3) concerns that homeowners may be inappropriately asked to purchase an amount of flood insurance that is several times the value of the actual property.

Introduction

This chapter examines the federal government's efforts to conduct a nationwide Flood Insurance Study (FIS) to obtain new flood-hazard data, publish more accurate, up-to-date flood-risk assessments and maps, and to require more homeowners to buy flood insurance if they live behind dams or levees. As part of the Federal Emergency Management Agency's (FEMA) map modernization program, the agency has implemented a policy to verify the certification status of all levees currently depicted on flood insurance rate maps (FIRMs). Currently, if FEMA agrees that a levee shown on a government-issued FIRM can withstand a 100-year flood—that is, a flood that has only a 1% chance of happening in any given year—then the homes and businesses protected by the levee are not considered to be in the floodplain.[1] This means homeowners living there do not have to buy federal flood insurance. Homeowners may be affected if FEMA decertifies the levee.

The National Flood Insurance Program

Floods and severe storms are among the most costly kind of weather and climate disaster in the United States. The standard homeowners insurance policy generally excludes losses caused by flood. This gap in coverage is usually filled with the purchase of flood insurance from the National Flood Insurance Program (NFIP) in communities where certain required flood control activities have been undertaken. In 1968, Congress established the NFIP to provide insurance for property damage due to flooding. The NFIP remains the regime in which the federal government provides insurance, maps the floodplains, and oversees the national regulation of the land use ordinances.

Under the NFIP, the federal government makes subsidized flood insurance available to homeowners through a network of private insurance companies (called Write-Your-Own companies) in communities that agree to implement and enforce minimum national standards for regulating new development in floodplains. Land use controls are usually adopted to steer new construction away from high-risk locations and to otherwise mitigate construction in hazardous zones.

In addition, the federal government studies flood hazards and publishes floodplain maps that show the probability of flooding in a particular area within 100 years. This regulatory standard then requires raising of the first floor of new construction above the elevation of the 100-year storm. In the highest-risk zones, where water moves with velocity, there would normally be no construction, and any new construction would not get the subsidized rates but would pay full actuarial rates. Lenders are required to protect the collateral (the structure) with flood insurance if the mortgage is federally guaranteed and the structure is in a high-risk flood zone.

Flood Insurance, Maps, and Floodplain Management

In the wake of Hurricane Katrina in 2005, three sets of problems have emerged with respect to flood maps, the insurance program, and the increased frequency of extreme weather events across the country, along with increased likelihood of devastating floods, including the Midwest flood in 2008.

- Recent catastrophic flooding revealed that FEMA floodplain maps were sometimes over 20 years old and seriously outdated, based on old evaluations of levees and river conditions.
- Losses from major floods have been compounded by over-reliance on levees and other strategies for taming rivers, which encouraged development in flood-prone areas. Rivers and streams have been increasingly altered by dams, levees, and other structures intended to increase inland navigation and flood control. In some cases, levees built 50 years ago for agricultural purposes are now expected to function as a residential or urban levee. Floods in 1993 and 2008 breached or topped these levees, which were not built to handle such floods of historic proportions.
- Experts generally agree on a need to expand to "residual risk" areas the requirement that lenders require borrowers to purchase flood insurance. These are areas that are subject to flooding by the 0.2%-annual chance flood (500-year flood), areas subject to coastal storm surge floods, and areas that would be subject to flooding but for the presence of flood control structures such as levees, dams, and other man-made structures—the so-called "natural 100-year floodplain."

The 111th Congress could opt to consider various comprehensive proposals to reform and modernize the NFIP.[2] A key part of that reevaluation would likely be the costs of floodplain remapping and expanding mandatory flood insurance purchase requirements to 500-year flood zones.

Flood Risk Assessment and Mapping

As part of its administration of the NFIP, FEMA identifies the nation's flood risks, establishes appropriate risk zone determinations, and reflects these determinations accurately on FIRMs. Flood maps generally delineate both high-risk zones, called special flood hazard areas (SFHAs),[3] and low-to-moderate risk zones with a less than 1% annual chance of flooding. FEMA maintains an inventory of roughly 106,000 maps. Accuracy is an essential component of the NFIP, and this requires the updating of maps to reflect natural and human-induced changes in the land surface within the floodplains. Flood maps serve a wide range of uses, including local planning, emergency preparedness and response, and natural resource management. FIRMs are also used by lending institutions and insurance companies to calculate flood insurance rates and establish who is required to comply with mandatory flood insurance purchase requirements.

According to the Government Accountability Office, 50% of the NFIP's roughly 106,000 maps were more than 15 years old in April 2008, and another 8% were 10 to 15 years old.[4] Outdated flood maps could give homeowners a false sense of security since the maps might not show their property being located in a flood risk zone. Developers could construct properties in flood risk areas not identified on outdated or inaccurate flood maps. Finally, outdated flood maps impair the actuarial soundness of the FEMA's flood insurance program.

In 2003, at the urging of Congress and in collaboration with state and local partners, FEMA launched a five-year public awareness and map modernization program (Map Mod) to convert existing paper FIRMs into more accurate digital flood insurance rate maps (DFIRMs).[5] In 2005, acting on direction from Congress and feedback from the U.S. Government Accountability Office, the Department of Homeland Security's Inspector General, and other stakeholders, FEMA undertook a mid-course evaluation of its flood map modernization program.[6] This comprehensive evaluation found that there was a need for greater flexibility in determining flood areas to be mapped, particularly areas behind levees.

A key challenge in Map Mod has been to obtain high-accuracy digital land-surface elevation data. A solution was light detection and ranging

(LIDAR) technology, which is based on remote-sensing laser measurements collected from aircraft. Both sets of data—base map imagery and base flood elevation data—are imputed into the National Elevation Dataset that the U.S. Geological Survey (USGS) maintains in support of FEMA's flood map modernization goals.

As part of the Map Mod program, FEMA initiated a nationwide flood insurance study (FIS) to update flood-hazard data and to reflect accurately the flood hazard and risk in "levee-impacted" areas on DFIRM. According to FEMA, the primary goals of the FIS and DFIRM are to (1) incorporate available updated flood hazard information, as well as revisions effected by letters of map revisions (LOMRs) issued by FEMA since the latest FIS reports and FIRMs were published; (2) convert the base flood elevation data from the National Geodetic Vertical Datum of 1929 to the North American Vertical Datum of 1988; and (3) upgrade the FIRMs to a geographic information system (GIS) database format to set the stage for follow-up detailed engineering studies and restudies and to enable support for GIS analyses and other digital applications.

Residual Flood Risk of Levees

As part of FEMA's Map Mod program, FEMA has also implemented a policy to verify the certification status of all levees currently depicted on FIRMs as meeting design, operation, and maintenance standards for protection against the 1%-annual-chance flood.

The regulatory requirements for accrediting levees as providing base flood protection on FIRMs are found in Title 44 of the Code of Federal Regulations (CFR), Section 65.10 (44 CFR 65.10). These criteria include design criteria (e.g., freeboard, closures, embankment protection, embankment and foundation stability, settlement, interior drainage), operation, and maintenance. FEMA has specified levees to be built to withstand storm surges that rise three feet above the base flood elevation.

On August 22, 2005, FEMA issued Procedure Memorandum No. 34 to clarify that it is the community or levee system owner's responsibility to provide data and documentation to show that a levee system meets 44 CFR Section 65.10 requirements.[7] A levee accreditation designation allows a community and its structures to be removed from SFHA status. Levee accreditation means a community could be exempt from both flood insurance purchase requirements and local land-use restrictions.

Technical Criteria for Levee Certification

FEMA does not conduct a detailed physical inspection of levees to determine whether and how the flood control project or system will perform in a flood event. Rather, officials from FEMA's regional office typically meet with county and local community officials to put together a levee accreditation plan that outlines a process and time line to submit the levee certification data to FEMA that coincides with FIS and DFIRM schedules for the county.

For a levee system to become accredited, the community or levee owner seeking recognition must provide FEMA with certain data and documentation showing that the levee is (1) designed to withstand forces associated with the 1% annual chance flood (height, stability, and embankment protection); (2) adequate in terms of freeboard (e.g., minimum levee height is 3-4 feet above design flood state); (3) all closure devices function property; (4) operation and maintenance plans are adequate and in place; and (5) interior drainage systems (pumps and canals) are functioning. The documentation for accreditation is usually prepared by a registered professional engineer who knows FEMA's flood insurance study guidelines or by a federal agency (e.g., the U.S. Army Corps of Engineers (USACE)) with levee design and construction qualifications.

FEMA's accreditation is not a guarantee of performance of the levee. It is only a statement that data and documentation submitted to the agency is accurate and the analysis and design were performed correctly and in accordance with sound engineering practices and FEMA guidelines.[8] If a levee is not certified, FEMA has the power to designate the area protected by the levee as being in a SFHA, which forces homeowners in the residual risk area to purchase flood insurance as a condition of receiving a federally insured mortgage. Non-accredited levees are shown on flood maps as not providing protection from a base flood.

Provisionally Accredited Levee Systems[9]

FEMA's accreditation criteria are fairly direct. Communities and levee owners either provide all data to support that a given levee system complies with the requirements in 44 CFR 65.10—or they do not.[10]

To minimize the impact of mapping areas behind levees on the Map Mod goals, FEMA issued on September 25, 2006, Procedure Memorandum No. 43, "Guidelines for Identifying Provisionally Accredited Levees," to provide guidance on issuing preliminary and final effective DFIRMs, while providing communities/levee system owners with 24 months to compile and submit the data and documentation required to show compliance with 44 CFR Section

65.10. PM No. 43 established the concept of Provisionally Accredited Levee (PAL) systems.[11] On March 16, 2007, FEMA issued a revised version of PM No. 43 to clarify the procedures that FEMA and its mapping partners are to follow for federal and non-federal levee projects.

FEMA has essentially given levee owners additional time to submit evidence of the levee's status. In order for a levee to be provisionally accredited, the community or levee owner must commit to FEMA in writing to submit the full Section 65.10 compliance documentation for the levee within 24 months of the signed agreement. During the 24-month period of PAL, areas behind the levee are mapped as having a moderate flood risk and designated as a PAL. If, however, the area does not meet FEMA's criteria, the map will show the area as a high-risk zone, or a SFHA.

The 24-month PAL period has now expired for most communities. This situation presents a challenge for many local community residents and local officials, as well as their congressional representatives. Some Members of Congress have considered legislative options to extend the 24-month PAL period. Others have proposed providing explicit federal funding to local communities to fund the cost of securing FEMA accreditation.

On April 24, 2009, FEMA issued Procedural Memorandum 53, "Guidelines for Notifying and Mapping of Expiring Provisional Accredited Levee Designations," that provides guidelines for notification of communities/levee system owners regarding expiring PAL designations and for mapping of accredited and de-accredited levee-impacted areas after the PAL period expiration.[12] Under the new guidelines, FEMA's regional offices will send out (during the 24-month PAL period), two letters—90 days and 30 days before expiration—to the chief executive officer of all affected communities, as well as to the state levee safety official, the USACE district office, and the district offices of U.S. senators and representatives in those affected areas. FEMA's regional offices are authorized to determine if the PAL system will be accredited or de-accredited. FEMA must begin a remapping of the area immediately upon determining that the PAL system is to be accredited or de-accredited. This process must last at least 18 months before a preliminary DFIRM can be issued that reflects either the newly designated accredited or de-accredited levee system.[13]

FEMA will not grant an extension to the 24-month PAL period. However, PM No. 53 outlines procedures that essentially allow communities and levee system owners additional time to provide the 44 CFR Section 65.10 compliance data and documentation submittals to FEMA before the DFIRM is final and becomes effective.

MANDATORY PURCHASE REQUIREMENTS

Under the National Flood Insurance Act of 1968,[14] as amended by the Flood Disaster Protection Act of 1973[15] and the National Flood Insurance Reform Act of 1994[16] regulated lending institutions,[17] federal agencies,[18] and secondary market entities[19] involved in mortgage loan transactions cannot make, increase, extend, or renew any loan secured by improved real estate or a mobile home in any area that has been designated by the Administrator of FEMA as a SFHA unless the building or mobile home or any personal property securing the loan is covered by the required amount of flood insurance.

If the property is not located in an SFHA, but instead in a low-to-moderate flood risk area, federal law does not require flood insurance; however, it is recommended since historically about one in four flood claims have come from these low-to-moderate risk areas. In addition, the mandatory flood insurance purchase requirement does not apply to loans on state-owned property covered under an adequate policy of self-insurance satisfactory to the Administrator of FEMA or to loans with an original principal balance of $5,000 or less, and having an original repayment term of one year or less.

Pursuant to federal flood insurance laws and regulations, the amount of flood insurance that must be purchased depends on several factors, primarily the amount of financial assistance,[20] the unpaid principal balance (UPB) on loans secured by real property in an SFHA, and the maximum amount of insurance available through NFIP.[21] The formula for determining the correct amount of flood insurance is fairly straightforward, but in practice it has generated considerable ambiguity and confusion among financial institutions, particularly as it relates to determining the "insurable value" of the building using the new FEMA guidelines that imposes a claims recovery limit standard of 100% replacement cost value (RCV).[22] The old FEMA guidelines are based on appraised value minus the value of the land.

Despite efforts by FEMA to clarify the definition of the mandatory flood insurance purchase requirement, considerable confusion still exists among lenders. FEMA recommends that lenders seek guidance from financial institution regulatory authorities with respect to determining insurable value. The problem is that neither the 1973 and 1994 Acts (see **Appendix A**) nor NFIP's implementing regulations defines the term "insurable value." Consequently, there are inconsistencies in how the insurable value is determined by the various lenders and the amount that a borrower could possibly collect under a General Property Form which is used in insuring nonresidential structures.[23] Definitions used by lenders vary; some define the insurable value as "appraised value minus land" while others refer to it as "100% of the full replacement cost value (RCV) including the supporting structure." One may argue that there is a need for one consistently applied standard for determining the insurable value. This issue is being addressed by the new guidance, "Loans in Areas Having Special Flood Hazards: Interagency Questions and Answers Regarding Flood Insurance" (Flood Q&A), published by the federal financial regulatory agencies (see discussion in **Appendix A**).

The September 2007 "Mandatory Purchase of Flood Insurance Guidelines" (FEMA guidelines) were designed to address the ambiguities in determining the appropriate flood insurance purchase obligations.[24] However, the new reference in the FEMA guidelines to 100% RCV in the context of NFIP's recovery limits on the NFIP's Standard Flood Insurance Policy (SFIP) has raised questions from lenders on how to determine RCV when calculating the amount of insurance that must be obtained. Although federal law and regulation impose a minimum amount of flood insurance that each loan must have, it does not prevent lenders from requiring that each loan be insured up to the NFIP's recovery limits (100% RCV) subject to the maximum coverage available through the program. Lenders can also require that personal property within a structure located in a SHFA be insured if the property secures all or part of a loan.

Determining the Appropriate Amount of Flood Insurance

The NFIP Guidelines require flood insurance to be purchased in an amount equal to the lesser of

- the maximum amount of coverage available for the type of building,
- the outstanding principal balance of the loan, or
- the full insurable value of the property, which is the same as 100% of the replacement cost value (excluding the appraised value of the land).[25]

The NFIP pays flood damage losses on the basis of replacement cost value for primary residences where the insured has purchased insurance of up to at least 80% of the replacement cost of the structure.[26] This is done to ensure sufficient resources to pay the full cost of repair or replacement without deduction for depreciation. The various federal agencies that oversee lending institutions generally follow FEMA's *Purchase of Flood Insurance Guidelines* (including recovery limits) but are free to develop their own regulations.

For practical purposes, however, given Fannie Mae's traditional role as a major secondary market for residential mortgages, most mortgage lenders usually follow Fannie Mae's guidance when calculating the amount of insurance that must be obtained. According to Fannie Mae, "replacement cost value" refers to the cost of rebuilding a damaged property of the same size with the same amenities as the original structure. Fannie Mae requires that flood insurance for a first mortgage be the lesser of

- the amount required to compensate for any damage or loss on a replacement cost basis (or UPB if replacement cost coverage is not available), or
- the maximum insurance available from the NFIP.[27]

When UPB is the selected option, the minimum amount of flood insurance must be at least 80% of the RCV of the structure. However, if the UPB is less than 80% of the RCV, the required insurance coverage amount must still be at least 80% of the structure (market) value.

Because the NFIP flood insurance dwelling policy pays 100% of a loss on the basis of replacement cost only when the amount of insurance purchased is at least 80% of the replacement cost of the building, a lender must obtain coverage for at least 80% of replacement cost (the minimum amount required) in order to meet Fannie Mae's standards. This means replacement cost coverage is considered not available when the property is insured for less than 80% of its replacement cost. Coverage in a lesser amount would not meet the standard for replacement cost because it would be subject to the (20%) co-insurance payment.

In light of Fannie Mae's flood insurance standards, lenders typically will insist on flood insurance amounts of at least 80% of the replacement cost of the insurable value of the property—up to the maximum available under the NFIP—rather than the outstanding loan balance amount. Again, if the UPB is less than 80% of the replacement cost, the required insurance coverage amount must be at least 80% of the structure value. This is based on Fannie Mae's interpretation of FEMA's guidance. It is important to point out that the authority of FEMA remains limited to its statutory responsibility of administering the NFIP. In other words, FEMA does not have direct responsibility for enforcement of the mandatory flood insurance purchase requirements. This is the responsibility of the banks and other financial institutions.

As an illustration of Fannie Mae's interpretation of FEMA's regulatory standard, a borrower with a UPB of $100,000 on property with a replacement value of $300,000 would be required to purchase minimum flood insurance coverage equal to $240,000 (80% of $300,000), and not the outstanding loan value of $100,000. Thus, the borrower could find himself/herself paying for coverage that is substantially greater than the outstanding loan balance.

APPENDIX A. EVOLUTION OF FEDERAL FINANCIAL REGULATORY AGENCY REGULATION

Title V of the Riegle Community Development and Regulatory Improvement Act of 1994, which is also know as the National Flood Insurance Reform Act of 1994[28] (Reform Act), broadened the definition of "federal regulated lending institution" to include the Farm Credit Administration (FCA), thereby increasing the number of lending institutions subject to the mandatory flood insurance purchase requirement. The 1994 Reform Act applied flood insurance requirements directly to loans purchased by the Federal National Mortgage Association (Fannie Mae) and the Federal Home Loan Mortgage Corporation (Freddie Mac) and to agencies that provide government insurance or guarantees such as the Small Business Administration (SBA), Federal Housing Administration (FHA) and the Veterans Administration (VA).

Each federal regulatory agency was given the right to issue its own regulations to implement the mandatory flood insurance purchase requirement provisions in the 1973 and 1994 Acts. The six federal financial regulatory agencies exercise their rights by issuing substantially similar joint final regulations on August 29, 1996 (the Regulations)[29] and have coordinated and consulted with the Federal Financial Institutions Examination Council (FFIEC).[30] The Regulations establish the mandatory purchase requirements in the following way:

> A bank shall not make, increase, extend, or renew any designated loan unless the building or mobile home and any personal property securing the loan is covered by flood insurance for the term of the loan. The amount of insurance must be at least equal to the lesser of the outstanding principal balance of the designated loan or the maximum limit of coverage for the

> particular type of property under the Act. Flood insurance coverage is limited to the overall value of the property securing the designated loan minus the value of the land on which it is situated.[31]

Fannie Mae and Freddie Mac also established procedures to implement the NFIP's mandatory flood insurance purchase requirement.[32]

Despite the guidance provided by the Regulations, lenders still struggled with the lack of certainty and uniformity with the mandatory flood insurance provisions of the 1994 Reform Act. In 1997, the federal financial regulatory agencies responded to these concerns with the release of the *Loans in Areas Having Special Flood Hazard: Interagency Questions and Answers Regarding Flood Insurance*;[33] however, considerable ambiguity and confusion remained.

On May 25, 2006, Fannie Mae revised its existing mandatory flood insurance coverage requirements applicable to single and multi-family properties to the lowest of (1) the amount required to compensate for any damage or loss on a replacement cost basis (or unpaid principle balance if replacement cost coverage is not available); or (2) the maximum insurance available from the NFIP. This requirement is substantially similar to requirements issued by the NFIP; however, Fannie Mae tends to have stricter requirements for lenders that exceed the NFIP's three options. The Fannie Mae regulation requires that when the unpaid principal balance (UPB) is the selected option, flood insurance purchase amount must be at least 80% of the structure replacement cost. If the UPB is less than 80% of the replacement cost, the required insurance coverage amount must be at least 80% of the structure value.[34]

On March 21, 2008, in an effort to promote the consistent interpretation, application, and examination of bank regulatory obligations arising from implementation of the 1994 reform, the federal lending regulatory agencies, under the auspices of the FFIEC, proposed major revisions to the interagency questions and answers document.[35] The proposed changes were in areas such as second lien mortgages, construction loans and condominiums, the implementation of civil money penalties, loan syndications/participation, the imposition of new guidelines for handling discrepancies between flood zone descriptions in the flood determination form and the flood insurance policy, and a re-organization to make the guidance easier to use. On July 21, 2009, the agencies issued a modified version of the Flood Q&A after considering the comments received. Effective September 21, 2009, the agencies' modified Flood Q&A supersede the 1997 Interagency Questions and Answers and supplement other guidance or interpretations issued by the agencies and FEMA.[36]

The Federal Housing Finance Agency (FHFA) was created as a new, unified regulator for Fannie Mae, Freddie Mac, and the Federal Home Loan Banks under the Housing and Economic Recovery Act of 2008 (HERA).[37] On October 10, 2008, the FHFA requested public comments on the issuance of a proposed flood insurance regulation to codify the authority and responsibility of FHFA to oversee and enforce the statutory requirements affecting the operations of Fannie Mae and Freddie Mac.[38] Section 1161(e) of HERA amended section 102(f)(3)(A) of the Flood Disaster Protection Act of 1973 by replacing the Office of Federal Housing Enterprise Oversight (OFHEO) in the Department of Housing and Urban Development (HUD) with FHFA as the agency responsible for determining compliance of Fannie Mae and Freddie Mac's flood insurance responsibilities. The proposed regulation will supersede the OFHEO flood insurance regulations.[39]

APPENDIX B. GLOSSARY OF ACRONYMS

Glossary

ACV	Actual Cash Value
CFR	Code of Federal Regulations
DFIRM	Digital Flood Insurance Rate Map
FEMA	Federal Emergency Management Agency
FIRM	Flood Insurance Rate Map
FIS	Flood Insurance Study
GIS	Geographic Information System
GSE	Government Sponsored Enterprise
LIDAR	Light Detection and Ranging technology
LOMR	Letter of Map Revisions
LOMA	Letter of Map Adjustment
NFIP	National Flood Insurance Program
PAL	Provisionally Accredited Levee
RCV	Replacement Cost Value
SFHA	Special Flood Hazard Area
SFIP	Special Flood Insurance Policy
USGS	United States Geological Survey

UPB	Unpaid Principal Balance
USACE	U.S. Army Corp of Engineers

End Notes

[1] The 100-year concept is a probabilistic standard for an area within a floodplain that has a 1% or greater chance of flood occurrence within a given year. Such an event could actually happen twice in a year, while the average occurrence remains only once in a century.

[2] See CRS Report R40650, *National Flood Insurance Program: Background, Challenges, and Financial Status* , by Rawle O. King.

[3] Special Flood Hazard Areas (SFHAs) are defined as land areas on the FIRMs that are subject to inundation by a flood that has a 1% probability of being equaled or exceeded in any given year.

[4] U.S. Government Accountability Office, *Flood Insurance: FEMA's Rate-Setting Process Warrants Attention*, Report GAO-09-12, October 31, 2008, p. 18, located at http://www.gao.gov/products/GAO-09-12.

[5] The three components of the DFIRMs are (1) the base map imagery that provides land surface information such as location of streams, roads, and buildings; (2) base elevation data which is superimposed on top of the land surface information to provide 3-dimensional information; and (3) engineering analysis such as data and models of stream and river flows. Base map imagery is generally obtained from aerial and satellite photographs.

[6] See Federal Emergency Management Agency, "Flood Map Modernization: Mid-Course Adjustment Executive Overview," March 27, 2006, located at *http://www.fema.gov* /pdf/fhm/mm_mcaovr.pdf.

[7] See *http://www.fema.gov/library/viewRecord.do?id=2367*.

[8] 44 CFR 65.2(b).

[9] FEMA's Procedure Memorandums are accessible at http://www.fema.gov/plan/ prevent/fhm/lv_fpm.shtm.

[10] Under 44 CFR Part 67, communities may appeal the proposed base flood elevations on a map if they submit technical or scientific evidence refuting those elevations.

[11] See http://www.fema.gov/library/viewRecord.do?id=2511.

[12] See http://www.fema.gov/library/viewRecord.do?id=3632.

[13] Ibid.

[14] P.L 90-448, 82 Stat. 476.

[15] P.L. 93-234, 87 Stat. 975.

[16] P.L. 103-325, 108 Stat. 2257-2260.

[17] *A regulated lending institution* is any bank, savings and loan association, credit union, farm credit bank, federal land bank association, production credit association, or similar institutions subject to the supervision of a federal financial regulatory agencies including the Board of Governors of the Federal Reserve system (FED), the Farm Credit Administration (FCA), Federal Deposit Insurance Corporation (FDIC), National Credit Union Administration (NCUA), Office of the Comptroller of the Currency (OCC), and the Office of Thrift Supervision (OTS).

[18] The federal agencies are: Small Business Administration (SBA), Veterans Administration, and Federal Housing Administration (FHA).

[19] Federal National Mortgage Association (Fannie Mae), the Federal Home Loan Mortgage Corporation (Freddie Mac) and the Government National Mortgage Association (Ginnie Mae) are considered federal agencies for purposes of flood insurance and are often referred to as government-sponsored enterprises (GSEs). These organizations support residential

housing ownership by providing liquidity to the residential mortgage market. Congress did not make the Federal Agriculture Mortgage Corporation (Farmer Mac), another GSE, subject to flood insurance requirements.

[20] Financial assistance means any form of direct, insured, or guaranteed loan, any form of grant, or any form of direct or indirect assistance extended by a federal agency.

[21] For single-family and two-to-four family dwellings, the maximum amount of flood insurance available under the NFIP is $250,000; up to $500,000 in coverage is available for nonresidential buildings.

[22] See Federal Emergency Management Agency, National Flood Insurance Program, *Mandatory Purchase of Flood Insurance Guidelines*, (September 2007), located at http://www.fema.gov/good_guidance/download/10040.

[23] There are three different NFIP coverage forms—the general property form, the residential condominium association policy, and the dwelling form. The general property form covers other residential buildings of five families or more and nonresidential buildings. The residential condominium association policy covers the common elements and all structural items of the condominium units within a building. It also covers contents owned in common. The dwelling form can be used to cover single-family and multi-family dwellings.

[24] FEMA's National Flood Insurance Program, *Mandatory Purchase of Flood Insurance Guidelines*, September 2007, located at http://www.fema.gov/good_guidance/d wnload/10040.

[25] The statutory basis of FEMA's mandatory flood insurance purchase requirements are found at 42 U.S.C. 4012a(b)(3).

[26] In the case of nonresidential property, the recovery limit is calculated on an actual cash value (ACV) basis which accounts for depreciation in the property.

[27] Fannie Mae, *Announcement 06-05, Property Insurance Changes*, May 25, 2006, located at https://www.efanniemae.com/sf/guides/ssg/annltrs/pdf/2006/06-05.pdf.

[28] P.L. 103-325, 108 Stat. 2255.

[29] *Federal Emergency Management Agency*, "Loans in Areas Having Special Flood Hazards: Final Rule," *Federal Register*: August 29, 1996, vol. 61, No. 169, pp. 45683-45716, located at http://www.fema.gov/business/nfip/cfr.shtm. Individual agency rules are codified at 12 CFR Part 22 (OCC), 12 CFR Part 208 (Fed. Res), 12 CFR Part 339 (FDIC), 12 CFR Part 572 (OTS), 12 CFR Part 614 (FCA), and 12 CFR Part 760 (NCUA).

[30] The FFIEC was created under the Federal Financial Institutions Examination Council Act of 1978 (Title X of P.L. 95-630) as an interagency body that prescribes uniform principles, standards, and report forms for the federal examination of financial regulatory institutions and makes recommendations to promote uniformity in the supervision of financial institution.

[31] See, e.g., 12 CFR Part 339.3(a).

[32] See *Fannie Mae Form 4335: Property, Liability and Other Insurance Requirements*, May 2000, located at https://www.efanniemae.com/mf/loandocs/doc/3maxexpress/4335.doc. See also 12 C.F.R. Part 1773.

[33] FDIC Financial institution letter may be accessed from the FDIC's website located at https://www.fdic.gov/news/ news/financial/2007/index.html.

[34] See Fannie Mae 2007 Single Family Selling Guide, Part V, ch.4, § 403. For the flood insurance requirements currently in effect for Fannie Mae, see Fannie Mae 2009 Single Family Selling Guide, Part B, ch. B7-3-08.

[35] Office of the Comptroller of the Currency, Federal Reserve System, Farm Credit Administration, Office of Thrift Supervision, Farm Credit Administration, and National Credit Union Administration, "Loans in Areas Having Special Flood Hazards: Interagency Questions and Answers Regarding Flood Insurance," *Federal Register,* vol. 73, no. 56, March 21, 2008, pp. 15259-15278, located at http://www.fdic.gov/regulations/laws/federal /2008/08Noticemarch21.pdf.

[36] *Federal Register*, vol. 74, no. 138, July 21, 2009, pp. 35914-35947, located at http://edocket.access.gpo.gov/2009/ pdf/E9-17129.pdf.

[37] P.L. 110-289, 122 Stat. 2654.

[38] Federal Housing Finance Agency (FHFA), Office of Federal Housing Enterprise Oversight, Department of Housing and Urban Development, "Flood Insurance," *Federal Register*, vol. 73, no. 198, October 10, 2008, pp. 60198-60201, located at *http://www.fhfa.g* ov/webfiles/385/FloodInsuranceFR11509.pdf.

[39] 12 CFR Part 1773.

In: National and Mandatory Flood Insurance ISBN: 978-1-61209-126-6
Editors: A. Muñoz and M. Phillips

Chapter 4

POST-KATRINA INSURANCE ISSUES SURROUNDING WATER DAMAGE EXCLUSIONS IN HOMEOWNER'S INSURANCE POLICIES

Rawle O. King

SUMMARY

In the aftermath of Hurricanes Katrina and Rita in 2005, homeowners in Louisiana, Mississippi, and Alabama protested what they view as inappropriate obstacles to the payment of their property_ damage insurance claims. When insurance adjustors and damage experts assessed the properties damaged by the 2005 storms, they were faced with the issue of allocating damages between wind (a covered loss) and flood (an excluded loss). The delays and economic uncertainty that this activity has engendered have raised financial and legal issues for insurers, as well as homeowners and businesses along the Gulf Coast region.

The solution for some of the insureds has been to litigate with their insurers under a variety of legal theories with the objective of avoiding the standard "water damage" exclusion—a move that would arguably allow insureds to receive coverage for water damage under their homeowners' policies. Many of these theories rely on the principle that any ambiguity in the insurance policy should be construed in favor of the policyholder. In addition, even where the water damage exclusion is enforced, difficult factual and legal disputes have arisen relating to the allocation of damage between covered wind damage and excluded flood damage.

In the aftermath of the devastating 2005 hurricane season, three broad policy issues for Congress have emerged related to post-Katrina economic uncertainties: (1) the massive insured and uninsured property losses and their impact on Gulf Coast property insurance markets and rebuilding after Katrina, (2) assertions that insurers have shifted the cost of damages onto the federal flood program and U.S. taxpayers, and (3) unreliable government flood maps that are used in decision making by homeowners for purchasing insurance.

Post-Katrina insurance claims litigation and the economic uncertainty it generates for consumers and insurers raise concerns about the volatility in the legal environment in terms of post-event judicial interpretations in the scope of insurance coverage. What should be done to mitigate the economic consequences of future floods? Are the American people and policymakers ready to address perceived weakness in the U.S. floodplain management policy? Should the nation forgo development of its floodplains (a new policy initiative) or continue along the current path embodied in the NFIP? Insurance analysts have observed that a large percentage of those eligible to buy federally subsidized flood insurance do not. What could or should be done about this? These and other policy questions will be examined during congressional oversight hearings in the 111th Congress.

INTRODUCTION

Hurricane Katrina, the storm surges it produced, and the subsequent levee failures caused devastating flooding in communities located along the Gulf of Mexico Coast. Katrina's winds destroyed or substantially damaged many of the properties located on the Mississippi Gulf Coast, as well as property located further inland from the immediate coastal areas. Tens of thousands of homes and businesses in Louisiana, Mississippi, and Alabama were damaged as a direct result of Katrina's storm surge. Many thousands more homes were condemned and left empty due to exposure to days and even weeks of soaking in often-contaminated flood waters.

Modern homeowners' and business owners' policies are often issued on an "open perils" or "special causes of loss" basis which provides that all direct physical loss or damage to insured property is covered except as specifically excluded. Some policies are still issued on a "named perils" or "specified perils" basis by which the insurer promises to insure covered property only if damaged by listed perils and subject to certain exclusions. Under either approach, damage by wind is typically covered while water damage from flooding, wind driven water, storm surge, seepage or through openings in the building (not cause by other damage) is typically specifically excluded.

There are three main reasons that insurers utilize exclusions: (1) the excluded peril or property is more appropriately insured under a different insurance product or through an optional coverage (e.g., exclusion in property policies for earthquake and mobile equipment); (2) insurance is not an appropriate vehicle for transfer of a particular risk (e.g., exclusions in property policies for failure of appropriate maintenance); or (3) the peril or property presents an unacceptable hazard to the insurer (e.g., exclusions in property policies for nuclear or contamination event). The water damage exclusion is thought to be the result of the first and third reasons. For many homeowners and small businesses, the only explicit insurance coverage against flood damage is underwritten by the National Flood Insurance Program (NFIP), but homeowners have not participated in sufficient numbers for various reasons, as required by law.[1]

Because of water damage exclusions and underutilization of available NFIP coverage, a significant number of the thousands of properties damaged or lost through Hurricanes Katrina and Rita were uninsured. These storms have spawned numerous class actions and other litigation concerning insurance coverage for losses. Both uninsured and underinsured property owners have focused on the water damage exclusions in homeowners' policies, maintaining that they apparently should be made whole through government flood insurance, homeowners' insurance, some combination of both, or the government, depending on each person's particular insurance coverage.

For example, the Insurance Services Office (ISO) commercial policy wording (CP 10-30-04 02) with respect to the flood exclusion provides the following:

> *We will not pay for loss or damage caused directly or indirectly by any of the following. Such loss or damage is excluded regardless of any other cause or event that contributes concurrently or in any sequence to the loss....*

(1) *Flood, surface water, waves, tides, tidal waves, overflow of any body of water, or their spray, all whether driven by wind or not:*
(2) *Mudslide or mudflow;*
(3) *Water that backs up or overflows from a sewer, drain or sump; or*
(4) *Water under the ground surface pressing on, or flowing or seeping through;*
   (a) *Foundations, walls, floors or paved surfaces;*
   (b) *Basements, whether paved or not; or*
   (c) *Doors, windows or other openings.*

But if water, as described in g(1) through g(4) above, results in fire, explosions or sprinkler leakage, we will pay for the loss or damage caused by that fire, explosion or sprinkler leakage.

Insurers take the position that these policies do not provide coverage for water damage resulting from such events as levee breaches or storm surge because of the policy exclusion. For example, the standard homeowners' insurance policy language does not specifically identify "storm surge," but insurers insist that the breadth of the water damage exclusion encompasses such damage.

Insurance coverage disputes and litigation over the policy exclusions have ensued between policyholders and their insurers. The key coverage issue has been and will be whether damage or destruction to properties along the coastal regions was caused by winds (typically covered under homeowners' policies) or by the flooding accompanying the storm (typically excluded under homeowners' policies). With Katrina, the possibility exists that either wind or flood caused damage—either separately or working in combination. Disputes over causation are inevitable. Hundreds of millions and perhaps billions of dollars in potential insurance coverage will rest on the outcome of decisions rendered in the courts.

This chapter provides an analysis of post-Katrina insurance issues in the context of the magnitude and impact of flooding and the way private insurers settle claims under property policies when both covered and uncovered risks combine to cause a loss. The report does not provide legal advice, nor is it a definitive assessment of the applicable law in each jurisdiction.

THE ISSUES

Overview

Private insurers play a central role in the functioning of the U.S. economy not only because of their risk-transfer function, but also because of their ability to provide relatively easy access to sources of capital. Instability in the availability and price of coverage, interruptions in the payment of claims immediately after a disaster, and the large numbers of uninsured or underinsured Americans have led to pressure for government intervention in property insurance markets. In the wake of Katrina's massive flooding and uninsured property losses, specific concerns have been expressed in Congress not only about making sure that every insurance claim owed is paid, but also that there is a Gulf Coast insurance market after all the litigation is concluded.

In 1983, as a result of adverse court decisions in which insurers were forced to pay flood-related_ claims that insurers did not believe they were responsible to pay, the property and casualty insurance industry revised its policy language in the exclusions in homeowners' policies. Today, almost all homeowners' policies have a water damage exclusion with anti-concurrent causation language[2] which, according to insurers, should have eliminated coverage for flooding including from storm surge and levee breaches. Not all water is excluded, just the water damage described in the exclusion. There are still several instances in which water damage is covered, such as when the pipes in a home freeze and burst, when a roof is ripped off the home and rain water comes in, or the fire department hoses down the house.

Particular policy phrases and their interpretation frequently are at the center of insurance-based litigation. The central question is how the courts will interpret the water damage exclusion or whether they will rule in favor of the claimants, forcing insurers to pay billions of dollars to repair flood damage. Certain other insurance-related issues have arisen, such as concerns that some insurers inappropriately billed the federal flood insurance program for claims that should have been paid by the insurers' wind policies.[3]

Some Members of the 111th Congress support efforts to investigate the Katrina claims practices of insurance companies that contract with the National Flood Insurance Program.[4] During the 110th Congress, the House Committee on Financial Services, Subcommittee on Oversight and Investigation, held hearings on insurance claims payment processes in the Gulf Coast after the 2005 Hurricanes. In response to the hearings, the Government

Accountability Office (GAO) published a report that found that insurance coverage gaps and claims uncertainties can arise when coverage for hurricane damage is divided among multiple insurance policies.[5] GAO concluded that greater transparency and oversight of wind and flood damage determinations are needed.

Other Members of Congress support legislation that would create a federal catastrophe fund backed by state funds to shore up the private insurance industry in the event of a mega-catastrophe. Still other Members support the repeal of the insurance industry's limited federal antitrust exemption to address what they insist is an anti-competitive industry. The exemption from federal antitrust laws has allowed collaboration in the industry, such as development of standardized policy forms.[6]

The Louisiana, Mississippi, and Alabama Departments of Insurance, like those in other states, have a right of review and approve policy forms before use. As with all other states, Louisiana and Mississippi have for many years reviewed and approved flood and related water exclusions.

Departments of Insurance have also undertaken efforts to advise residents that most personal and_ commercial property insurance policies do not cover flood and that a national program (NFIP) is available to meet flood insurance needs. This frequent communication effort includes fact sheets and press releases (Louisiana—2002, 2003, 2004, 2005; Mississippi—2000, 2002; Alabama—2002, 2004, 2005).

In addition, the federal government through the NFIP has for years undertaken a multi-media campaign to advise homeowners and business owners that most insurance policies do not cover flood—but that federal coverage is available. For homeowners' insurance, federal flood insurance is typically less than $1,000 per year (although pricing varies depending on the value insured and location of the property). For businesses, the federal flood insurance premium is typically a couple of thousand dollars, again depending on the amount of coverage and location of the property.

Litigation between policyholders and their insurers over the interpretation of "water damage" exclusion and the "anti-concurrent causation" clauses could continue for months and even years. The outcome of legal disputes will likely determine how losses are eventually apportioned among the National Flood Insurance Program (NFIP), private insurers, individuals, and businesses.[7]

Impact of Hurricane Katrina on Insurance Markets

In the aftermath of Hurricanes Katrina and Rita, three broad issues have emerged related to post-Katrina economic uncertainties:

- the massive insured and uninsured property losses and their impact on Gulf Coast property insurance markets and rebuilding after Katrina;
- assertions that insurers have shifted the cost for damage to the federal flood program and FEMA for U.S. taxpayers to pay the bill—i.e., potentially huge uninsured property losses and the denial of thousands of Katrina wind claims where insurers invoked the "water damage exclusion" and "anti-concurrent causation" clause in homeowners' policies;
- unreliable government flood maps that are used by homeowners, lenders, and realtors to determine whether flood insurance was needed.

First, Hurricanes Katrina, Rita and Wilma resulted in massive property losses for both private insurers and the National Flood Insurance Program (NFIP). In addition, the total value of uninsured property damage and business interruption caused by Katrina has been estimated at $135 billion.[8] Congress has already appropriated $109 billion for disaster relief and recovery aid to affected communities, plus more than $8 billion in tax relief.[9]

Unprecedented losses in the NFIP have led to unprecedented borrowing from the U.S. Treasury. As of January 31, 2009, the NFIP debt to the Treasury was $18.9 billion, and must be repaid with_ interest. The Congressional Budget Office calculates that FEMA is unlikely to repay the funds borrowed to pay 2005 hurricane-related claims within the next 10 years.[10] Consequently, the 111th Congress may choose to pursue comprehensive reform and long-term reauthorization of the NFIP in order to address: (1) program's financial solvency; (2) indebtedness to the U.S. Treasury; (3) magnitude of uninsured flood damage due to the widespread noncompliance with the mandatory flood insurance purchase requirements; and (4) controversy surrounding the practice of contracting with private insurers for policy adjusting and servicing.

Second, Hurricane Katrina damaged or destroyed thousands of homes and businesses that were covered for wind damages, but not water damage. Insurers have reportedly denied thousands of Katrina wind claims by assigning all Katrina damages to flooding covered by the NFIP and not to their own windstorm policies. Insurers say they are simply invoking the "water damage" exclusion and "anti-concurrent causation" clause in homeowners' policies. Policyholder advocates claim insurers have a conflict of interest because they are able to shift the cost for damage to the federal flood program rather than to themselves. Further, insureds doubt whether FEMA provides proper oversight of NFIP's Write Your Own (WYO)[11] insurers to ensure they are fulfilling their contractual obligations to fairly adjust flood claims, particularly those involving combined wind and water damage. Finally, critics charge that, while the states have a role in regulating the claims adjusting process, the "Unfair Claims Practices" statutes are not being adequately enforced by the states.

On the other side of this issue, many homeowners who were eligible for low cost NFIP flood coverage (including those required by law to purchase it) declined this available coverage despite state and federal educational efforts. Many insurers—and several recent editorials—assert that policyholders' claims of flood coverage under homeowners' policies with flood exclusions are post-event rationalizations for poor personal planning decisions.

Researchers have suggested that millions of families are now living in flood-prone areas without adequate insurance protection. This is despite that fact that structures in areas with at least a 1% chance of flooding in any given year—the so-called "100-year" flood or Special Flood Hazard Areas (SFHAs)—are required to have flood insurance if they have a loan from a federally insured or regulated lender. The insurance must be in an amount of at least equal to the outstanding principal balance of the loan or the maximum available under the NFIP, whichever is less.[12] This requirement is based on two federal laws: the Flood Disaster Protection Act of 1973[13] and the National Flood Insurance Reform Act of 1994.[14]

According to a Rand Corporation nationwide study, about 49% of single-family homes in SFHA are covered by flood insurance (the market penetration rate), with substantial variations across_ geographic regions.[15] In addition, about 1% of homeowners in non-SFHAs purchase flood insurance coverage.[16] The purchase of flood insurance is voluntary outside SFHAs.

Researchers have explored factors influencing insurance purchase decisions.[17] They include the following:

- Millions of homeowners incorrectly believe that their standard homeowners' policies automatically provide coverage against flooding, when in fact an additional flood policy is needed.
- People have misperception of risk and tend to underestimate their chances of being disaster victims and do not purchase flood insurance.

They have difficulty dealing with probabilistic information for small likelihood events because they need a context in which to evaluate the data.[18] Homeowners might think it is not a good investment when comparing the insurance price of coverage per dollar against their estimate of the probability of total loss, which they assume approaches zero.

- There are economic disincentives to buying flood insurance because of "free" federal and charitable disaster assistance and the tax-deductibility of flood losses.[19] Property owners often believe that disaster relief (i.e., Small Business Administration (SBA) low interest loans and grants) will compensate them for flood losses.
- The NFIP can undercompensate for losses given the high property (and land) values for coastal properties and the NFIP's maximum coverage of $250,000 for structure and $100,000 for contents.
- Property owners sometimes self-protect or self-insure—a substitute for formal insurance—by, for example, elevating their property above the base flood elevation (BFE), which serves to reduce both the probability of loss and the size of the potential costs.
- Homeowners might simply cancel their flood coverage without lenders taking action.
- Homeowners with mortgages issued by non-federally regulated lenders are not subject to the mandatory flood purchase requirements.

In response to low levels of compliance with the mandatory purchase requirements and the financial challenges facing federal insurance program, some insurance market analysts have proposed an overhaul of the NFIP to address these and other programmatic issues.[20] Although FEMA does have an interest in ensuring high levels of compliance, the agency must rely on federally regulated lenders, government sponsored enterprises (GSEs), and federal agencies that provide financial assistance for construction and acquisition of property in SFHAs to implement and monitor compliance with the mandatory purchase requirement. Some propose requiring all U.S. homeowners to purchase flood insurance, possibly the way liability insurance is required for automobile owners.

Third, thousands of residents along the Gulf Coast who relied on government flood maps to determine who must buy flood insurance were arguably unaware of their actual flood risk and uninsured when Hurricanes Katrina, Rita, and Wilma struck. An issue for the 111th Congress, therefore, might be to decide what to do about flood maps that may be incorrectly measuring risk and, therefore, not capturing the nation's exposure to flood risk. Critics of FEMA's flood map modernization efforts say these activities have been underfunded and lack focus.

Many people in Hurricane Katrina's path did not have flood insurance because, according to government flood maps, they were not in a floodplain and did not need coverage.[21] On October 18, 2005, the Department of Homeland Security's Inspector General released a report that raised concerns about the accuracy of flood maps.[22] The report concluded that outdated flood maps placed homeowners and residents at physical and financial risk because many people living in high-risk areas did not know of the dangers and, therefore, might not have chosen to participate in the NFIP.

Again, according to Rand Corporation, about one-third of all flood claims occur outside of SFHAs, yet only 1% of property owners residing in these areas purchase flood insurance from the NFIP. Communities in harm's way might not be adequately enforcing strong building codes or land use zoning ordinances, which would have reduced the amount of wind-related damage.

In the case of New Orleans—a city that experienced massive flooding and an historic 29-foot storm surge—FEMA flood maps incorrectly made the assumption that levees and flood walls would withstand the storm surge and protect the residents from flooding.[23] Many property owners in Katrina-impacted areas outside government-designated flood zones whose homes were destroyed were not subject to the mandatory purchase requirement and, therefore, did not have adequate coverage. Efforts are underway at FEMA under its flood map modernization program to develop accurate digital flood plain maps that are consistent in terms of data collection standards_ and analytical methods.

Post-Katrina Economic Uncertainty for Policyholders and Insurers

In the aftermath of Hurricanes Katrina and Rita, thousands of homeowners in Louisiana, Mississippi, and Alabama face significant obstacles in getting their property damage insurance claims paid. When insurance adjustors and damage experts assessed properties damaged by the 2005 hurricanes, they were faced with the issue of allocating damages between wind (a covered loss) and flood (an excluded loss). The ambiguity and economic uncertainty that this activity has engendered has raised financial and legal issues for insurers, as well as homeowners and businesses along the Gulf Coast region. The solution for some of the insureds has been to litigate with their insurers, seeking to declare the "water damage exclusion" clause in their policies unenforceable—a move that would arguably then allow insureds to receive coverage for flood damage under their homeowners' policies. Allocating damages between covered wind damages and excluded flood damages has become a question of fact to be decided by the courts.

Issues of Contention

Insurers attempt to separate the wind damage (covered) from the flood damage (excluded) through physical examination of the location. In many areas of New Orleans, for example, the house contains a clear water-line with no or minimal roof damage. Along the Mississippi coast, many homes are completely destroyed with only a slab remaining. In those cases, the factual investigation turns on an analysis of weather conditions and the construction of the home to determine the extent of wind damage that occurred prior to the destruction of the home by excluded storm surge. Policyholders and insurers can have different views on these facts which result in litigation.

From the industry's perspective, claims are settled in the same manner they always have been with regard to the water damage exclusion that they assert has been well known among homeowners and state regulators for years. Insurers have argued that they settle claims fairly and in accordance with policy language and the historical treatment in court cases of storm surge associated with flooding during a hurricane. This is why, insurers insist, the federal government offers flood insurance. In addition, insurers note that they did not cover, and therefore price, the flood risk in the homeowners' policies, and hence did not set aside appropriate loss reserves to pay such claims.[24] Further, insurers maintain that the uncertainty associated with the court's *ex post* re-interpretation of insurance policy terms and language substantially increases their risk—i.e., paying flood insurance claims after the loss without actuarially accounting for this event before the loss could jeopardize their financial solvency. If they raise rates to reflect the increased risk, their customers will pay more for coverage that is now provided by the NFIP.

Policyholders and their advocates have charged that insurers rely upon the "flood exclusion" and anti-concurrent causation policy language to not pay claims on homes damaged by a combination of wind and flood. From their perspectives, insistence on the unenforceability of the "flood exclusion" and the anti-concurrent clause is consistent with "reasonable expectation" since they thought they had "full protection."

Post-Katrina insurance claims litigation and the economic uncertainty it generates for consumers and insurers have raised at least four interrelated policy issues for the 110th Congress: insurance coverage disputes; disaster and the law; flood plain policy; and insurance reforms.

Insurance Coverage Disputes

There may be congressional oversight and investigations into the handling of Katrina-related insurance claims, and possible legislative efforts to modify the industry's antitrust exemption under the McCarran-Ferguson Act of 1945[25] and state supervision and regulation of the business of insurance. Members of the 111th Congress have the option to address the volatility in the legal environment in terms of post-event judicial interpretations in the scope of insurance coverage and legislative or regulatory "lock-ins" of capacity in the months and even years after a storm. After Katrina and Rita, for example, in states like Florida and Louisiana, the insurance commissioners declared a state of emergency in the state's insurance market and suspended certain statutes and regulations regarding policy cancellations, non-renewals, reinstatements, and claim filings. These emergency declarations have had the effect of "locking in" the investor capital that stands behind the policies sold in the state. Some insurance experts have suggested that legal and regulatory volatility tends to discourage rather than encourage the retention and expansion of capital commitments in the affected states.

Disasters and the Law

Katrina demonstrates apparent gaps in the legal system and its ability to respond to events of this magnitude. This issue is important if communities are to be able to rebuild and recover in a timely manner after a major catastrophe. In the short term, Congress might consider oversight and investigation hearings into post-Katrina insurance claims issues and the regulatory impact this could have on the insurance market. In the long term, businesses, including the insurance industry, rely on a predictable legal regime that will operate efficiently in an emergency situation. In anticipation of another Katrina-sized natural disaster, Congress has the option to consider the enactment of a nationwide body of "disaster law" so the nation might be better prepared to rebuild and recover after a major catastrophe.[26]

U.S. Floodplain Management Policy

What should be done and not done to recover from flood damage and mitigate the consequences of future floods? The aftermath of a disaster often presents the opportunity to address multiple long-standing problems. After Hurricane Katrina, the floodplain policy response seems to have been to build "bigger and better" flood protections systems—i.e., take a nationwide inventory of the structural flood controls (levees), reinforce and strengthen them, and expand requirements for insuring residual risks behind levees and dams. History (1920s-1960s and 1993 Midwest floods) has showed that relying on structural means of controlling floods, such as building levees and dams, is not always the best flood control policy. Two broad policy options have been suggested that would (1) surrender land to the water, a new idea that would require forgoing development of floodplains and property buyouts; or (2) continue along the current path embodied in the NFIP_ (i.e., risk assessment or mapping, floodplain management, and insurance protection), but strengthen zoning laws and construction standards, modernize flood maps, and enforce existing mandatory flood insurance purchase requirements.

Insurance Reforms

A large percentage of those eligible to buy federally subsidized flood insurance do not purchase the coverage. The NFIP subsidizes insurance rates for about 26% of policies, generally high-risk buildings built before NFIP floodplain regulations were established in their community. As a long-standing public policy, the federal government forgoes significant premium income because of policy subsidies. Moreover, losses associated with subsidized properties account for 25% to 30% of all claims losses. What is the solvency and regulatory impact of massive Katrina-related flood losses on the NFIP? How effective has the program's mandatory flood insurance purchase requirement been in increasing market penetration and reducing future flood losses?

INSURANCE POLICY LANGUAGE AND COVERAGE

Private insurers generally do not cover the flood hazard because of the problem of adverse selection,[27] and the perceived unprofitability and volatility of this line of insurance due to the absence of tools for technical risk rating or portfolio diversification. Since 1968, this gap in coverage has been filled by the purchase of federally subsidized flood insurance. Many homeowners incorrectly believe that their standard homeowners policies automatically provide coverage against flooding, when in fact an additional flood policy will be needed.

This section provides an analysis and comparison of both federal flood insurance and the NFIP's standard homeowners' insurance policy, and the nature and types of the insuring clauses, including the "water damage" exclusion provision.

Federal Flood Insurance

Federal flood insurance is available to residents only in communities that agreed to institute floodplain management strategies designed to reduce future flood losses. The federal government established certain minimum building and development standards for floodplain construction that the communities have to adopt in order to participate in the NFIP. Under the National Flood Insurance Act of 1968,[28] the federal government is required to map the nation's floodplain. In order to do so, FEMA determines flood risk through various sources specific to each community. This flood risk information is then delineated by zones on Flood Insurance Rate Maps (FIRMs).[29]

The area of flood hazards on these maps is the Special Flood Hazard Area (SFHA), which is defined as an area of land that experiences a 1% chance of being flooded in any given year (also known as the base flood or 100-year flood).

Standard Flood Insurance Policy (SFIP)

The NFIP offers three Standard Flood Insurance Policy (SFIP) forms: Dwelling Policy; General Property Policy; and Residential Condominium Building Association Policy. The *Dwelling Policy* is used to insure residential structures and their contents and is issued to homeowners (including those in condominium units, manufactured mobile/trailer homes, townhouse structures, and timeshares), residential renters, or owners of residential buildings containing two to four units. The Dwelling Form offers coverage for building property, up to $250,000, and personal property (contents), up to $100,000. Contents coverage must be purchased separately.

The *General Property Policy* is issued to owners of residential buildings with five or more units, owners or lessees of nonresidential structures, such as hotels, apartment buildings, schools, commercial structures, cooperative associations, and their contents. Coverage is available up to $500,000 for non-residential buildings and their contents.

The *Residential Condominium Building Association Policy* (RCBAP) is issued to residential condominium building associations to cover the entire building under one policy. The policy covers all units, improvements within the units, and personal property owned in common. Eligible structures under the RCBAP include high-rise and low-rise condominium buildings and condominium associations.

The SFIP is not a *guaranteed replacement cost policy* that pays the to rebuild regardless of the limit of liability in the event of a total loss. Instead, the SFIP policies pay the replacement cost of actual damages, up to the policy limit. In other words, flood insurance does not pay more than the policy limit.

NFIP'S Definition of a Flood

The NFIP defines a flood as

> general and temporary condition of partial or complete inundation of two or more acres of normally dry land area or of two or more properties from: overflow of inland or tidal waters, unusual and rapid accumulation or runoff of surface waters from any source, mudflow, or collapse or subsidence of land along the shore of a lake or similar body of water as a result of erosion or undermining caused by waves or currents of water exceeding anticipated cyclical levels.

The SFIP covers physical damage to the building or personal property "directly" caused by a flood. It does not cover: damage caused by moisture, mildew or mold; loss of currency and valuable papers such as stock certificates; living expenses such as temporary housing; and, financial losses caused by business interruption or loss of use of insured property.

Standard Homeowners' Insurance

The property insurance industry uses standardized policy language to provide uniformity in coverage and consistency in legal outcomes. The basic forms are developed and written by the Insurance Services Office Inc. (ISO).[30] The standard homeowners' insurance (HO) policy that ISO publishes combines various personal insurance protections which can include losses on the home, its contents, loss of its use (additional living expenses), as well as liability coverage in the event the homeowner is sued and found legally responsible for damages.

There are seven types of ISO standardized HO forms in general and consistent use. Of these, HO-3 is the most common policy, followed by HO-4 and HO-6. Others that are less used are HO-1, HO-2, HO-5, and HO-8. The HO-3 is a special homeowners policy—called *open-perils*—that covers all perils except those specifically excluded by the policy such as earthquakes, floods, *Acts of God*, or war. Special insurance can be purchased for these possibilities, including flood insurance and earthquake insurance. The HO policy might also contain options, called *riders*, *floaters*, or *endorsements,* that can provide additional coverages for such items as art or coin collections for an additional premium.

State insurance departments are responsible for reviewing and approving all insurance policy forms and rates before the policy can be lawfully used by an insurer. The approval process includes an examination of every word, sentence, and paragraph in the policy. Before the regulators are given the policy form for approval, however, it is standard practice in the industry for insurers to consult with actuaries and insurance underwriters to develop the policy language so that pricing is commensurate with the related coverage. Economic efficiencies are realized in this activity by utilizing certain industry organizations, like the ISO, to develop the specific provision in standard-form insurance policies and to file with the each state insurance department so that individual insurers can use them without expending money and time that would be required to get the policy forms approved in every state in which they operate.

By standardizing the HO policy, insurers hope that court interpretations of standard coverage forms provide consistent treatment of claimants. Thus, when a court determines the meaning of a word, phrase, or clause in a standard coverage form, that interpretation triggers a rewrite or adjustment to the policy language.

Insuring Clauses

Property and casualty (p/c) insurance policies are classified by causation, and contain in their insuring clauses the words, "loss caused by ... " or their equivalent. The insuring clause in the HO-3 policy is a statement of the promises the insurer makes to the insured as far as what perils and exposures are covered; it varies greatly from policy to policy. The problem is that when an insured cause (wind) joins with one or more additional causes (flood), which may be uninsured or may be insured under a separate contract, *concurrent causation* can be said to exist. It is this concurrent causation that has generated so much litigation surrounding the "wind v. flood" legal disputes. Litigation arises as to whether the damage was caused by an insured event or by an event which is either excluded from coverage or not within the scope of the policy.

Named-Perils v. Open-Perils Policies

Property policies come in several types, including commercial and homeowners. These policies are further divided by the type of risks insured: *named-peril risk* or *open-peril risk.* Named risk policies insure against physical loss or damage caused by various risks specified in the policy (e.g., fire, lightning, explosion, windstorm or hail, smoke, aircraft or vehicles, riot or civil commotion, vandalism, sprinkler leakage, sinkhole collapse and volcanic action).

Open-peril policies, on the other hand, insure against physical loss or damage caused by any risk that is not excluded or limited by the policy. The distinction between named-peril and open-peril policies becomes especially important in litigation. Under the named-peril policies, courts have held that a policyholder must first prove one or more of the named perils caused a loss. Insurers must then prove that the loss is excluded in the policy. Under an open-peril policy, the policyholder must prove damage occurred to the insured property. Insurers must establish that an excluded risk caused the loss.

In some litigation addressing the water damage exclusion, plaintiffs have contended that the water damage should be covered because it resulted from storm surge, which was not a specifically excluded peril. A recent federal court decision held that "storm surge" was within the policy definition of "flood" and the exclusion should apply.[31] In another case involving water damage but that specifically covered winds or hail, the court denied the insurer's motion to dismiss, hold that there was coverage for all damage caused by wind, and wind-driven rain, but that losses directly resulting from storm surge were excluded by the water damage exclusion.[32] Applying Mississippi law in the *Tuepker* case, the judge also held that the exclusionary language in the policy was invalid to the extent that it did not allow for consideration of the proximate cause (covered wind or uncovered water) of the insured's damage;[33] and further that, at trial, if the insured could prove its damage was sustained as a result of covered perils, its claim would be paid.[34]

Open-perils policies cover many perils not covered by named-perils policies; consequently, the open-perils policy provides broader coverage than a named-perils policy, and carries a higher premium. Whether the policy is open-perils or named-perils, however, the coverage it provides will have exclusions. Exclusions are an integral part of every insurance policy. The flood peril, in particular, is excluded from HO policies because it is unusual and requires a separate rating.

Water Damage Exclusion

In the event of hurricane-related flooding, the question of the cause of damage, whether wind *or* water or wind *and* water is of considerable importance.[35] The reason is that flood exclusion language has been a standard feature of homeowners' insurance policies since around 1968, when the federal government's National Flood Insurance Program (NFIP) was established. Homeowners' policies generally exclude coverage for flood damage. Insurers have not priced and, therefore, not collected premiums to pay for flood coverage.

An insurance policy usually specifies what causes—called "hazards" or "perils"—are covered. It also specifies what effects—called "losses" or "damages"—are covered and which perils and losses are excluded from coverage. The insurance industry defines an "exclusion" as a provision in an insurance policy that eliminates coverage for certain risks, people, property, classes, or locations. The insurance policy language that specifically excludes flooding is found in the "Perils Insured Against" and "Exclusions" section of the standard homeowners' policy.

CLAIMS ADJUSTMENT, CAUSATION, AND POLICY LANGUAGE INTERPRETATION

Two broad sets of post-Katrina claims-adjustment issues may be relevant to the 110th Congress. *First* is the alleged adverse impact on insureds of computerized claims settlement systems and products. Public interest advocacy groups have alleged that the insurance industry uses computer programs, such as "Colossus" sold by Computer Sciences Corporation (CSC) or "Claims Outcome Advisor" sold by the Insurance Services Office (ISO), to systematically underpay homeowners claims.[36] Their argument is that these systems allow insurers to calibrate the amount of savings they want to generate to the detriment of their insureds.

Claims adjustment under the NFIP is different from that in the private homeowners' insurance market. The adjustment of federal flood insurance claims is conducted by property and casualty insurers who write and service NFIP policies and claims under a contractual agreement with the NFIP's Write

Your Own (WYO) Program. Over 95% of NFIP's policies are written under this program. Private insurers enter into a "Financial Assistance Subsidy Arrangement" whereby they agree to issue flood policies in their own names and take responsibility for policy administration, claims processing, marketing, and sales. Private insurers handle all claims issued in their names, and adjust and settle flood loss claims consistent with their general claims practices. In adjusting flood insurance claims, which are binding upon the federal government, a WYO insurer is authorized to use staff adjusters or independent contractors selected and supervised by the company. The WYO insurer also determines when and how adjusters will be compensated for their work on flood claims.

WYO insurers typically receive an expense allowance for policies written and claims processed, and the federal government assumes total financial responsibility for underwriting losses. Insurers retain 15% of premiums written to cover commissions and salaries of agents and brokers. They are also reimbursed for marketing, operating, and administrative expenses. The expense ratio of the WYO appears to be about one-third of premiums.[37]

On January 18, 2006, the Collins Center for Public Policy issued a report that raised several specific concerns involving contracting with private insurance companies for NFIP policy claims adjusting and servicing. The issue paper indicated (1) WYO insurers had no financial incentive to adjust claims in the best interest of the NFIP because the federal government pays all claims, and (2) the existence of conflicts of interest for WYO insurers and their agents when they attempt to_ adjust possibly competing claims against flood insurance offered by NFIP, and claims against their own policies for wind or other coverage.[38]

Critics have charged that the NFIP appears to have few systemic checks and balances to ensure that it is being administered correctly. FEMA has responded to this charge by noting that WYO insurers are subject to certain standards and oversight as detailed in the NFIP's "Write Your Own Program Financial Control Plan Requirements and Procedures Manual." WYO insurers, for example, must comply with monthly financial and statistical transaction reporting requirements. They are subject to a review of operations—claims, underwriting, customer service, marketing, and litigation activities—every three years to assure that each company is meeting its performance objectives and adhering to program standards and policies. In addition, WYO insurers are subject to a "Biennial Claims Audit" every two years, and a "Claims Reinspection Program" that randomly reviews a percentage of WYO insurers' claims settlement practices.

Second is the issue of *causation* in the homeowners' claims adjustment process—a major source of insurance-coverage disputes between policyholders and their insurers: i.e., whether a loss was caused by winds (typically covered under homeowners' policies) or flooding accompanying the storm (typically excluded under homeowners' policies). Causation is the key factor involved in the water damage exclusion and the "wind versus flood" legal disputes in Louisiana and Mississippi.[39]

Homeowners insurance claims are typically paid if the loss is caused by a covered peril or, in the case of "all risk" (open-perils) policies, a peril that is not expressly excluded. If the loss is caused by multiple factors (mixed cases), such as wind that is covered and flood that is not, claims adjustment becomes more challenging. Both wind and flood, for example, might have worked together to cause the loss; one may have followed directly from the other, or the two may have arisen independently. In either case, the causal nature of the relationship between the perils has resulted in legal disputes between policyholders and their insurers. In order to resolve these mixed cases, the courts have developed various tests for situations in which an excluded peril and a non-excluded peril contributed to the loss, with the most prominent being the "efficient proximate cause" doctrine and the "concurrent causation" doctrine.[40]

Causation Battles over Hurricane Katrina Claims

The exact application of causation doctrines—"concurrent causation," "proximate cause," "efficient proximate cause," and "anti-concurrent causation"—in the context of Hurricane Katrina claims will depend on the type of insurance policy owned by the claimant, the facts of the claim,_ and the case law in the pertinent jurisdiction. Insurance lawyers have observed that every legally disputed case has unique features with different fact patterns and different levels and types of coverage that apply to each policyholder.

The next four sections examine causation doctrines or "rules of insurance policy interpretation" that could be used in understanding the tension between intended meaning in policy language and interpretation of certain provisions.

Concurrent Causation

Claimants' attorneys have focused considerable attention on finding ways to overcome decades of legal precedent supporting the flood exclusion. The principle of concurrent causation holds that if two causes combine to produce a loss or damage, and one of the two causes is excluded (e.g., flood) and the other is covered (e.g., windstorm), the loss will be covered absent policy wording to the contrary.[41] "Proximate cause" and "efficient proximate cause" are variations on "concurrent causation."

Proximate Cause

The proximate cause concept is particularly important in the "chain of causation" arguments involving wind versus flood claims following a major hurricane. Under the proximate cause concept, if a policy covers fire, not only is the direct damage by fire covered, but the collateral smoke damage—as well as damage from the water used by firefighters—is treated as a loss by fire. The key is that the damage must actually have been caused by the fire and any collateral damage that did not break the "chain of causation."

Proximate cause may impose limits on scope of legal liability because determining the cause of a loss can only be based on what is administratively possible and convenient, i.e., it may not be determinable with precision.

Efficient Proximate Cause

Given the uncertainty of determining actual "proximate cause," the efficient proximate doctrine is used by some courts to allocate losses when damage results from a combination of both covered and excluded causes. Thus, in the event of multiple causes for a loss, the efficient proximate cause doctrine allows payment under the policy if the non-excluded cause is the *dominant* cause of the loss (i.e., the one that sets the others in motion), notwithstanding that an excluded peril may have contributed to the loss.[42]

Attorneys and the courts frequently utilize the "but for" rule in determining how far back the chain of causation should go. The rule, as applied to the "wind-v.-flood" coverage dispute, says that "but for" the particular event (e.g., wind), the loss experienced by the plaintiff would not have occurred, even when the loss and the covered event are separated by a chain of events that include floods.

As in any insurance coverage litigation involving whether coverage should be available when both covered (wind) and excluded (flood) losses are part of a chain of events, there are differences of opinion on the proper scope of the efficient proximate cause doctrine, particularly whether the cause is considered a minor or major factor in producing the injury or damage.

Anti-Concurrent Causation Clauses

In response to the successful use of the concurrent causation arguments and the courts' reinterpretation of the flood exclusion language that has led to unanticipated exposures, insurers have sought to draft, file, and get state approval of policy language to make it as clear and unambiguous as possible that no damage due to flood is covered. Hoping to avoid the unexpected consequences of future adverse court decisions, insurers sought to implement industry-standard language designed to cover "all risks" not specifically excluded by the contract language. The "anti-concurrent causation" doctrine was designed to prevent the theory of concurrent causation from providing coverage for losses never intended to be covered by standard property insurance policies. Plaintiffs' attorneys, however, frequently argue that the exclusions are in violation of public policy.

Generally speaking, and notwithstanding some federal court decisions to the contrary, the efficient proximate cause doctrine has been adopted by the highest courts of Mississippi, Louisiana, and Alabama.[43] Courts in these three states have interpreted the doctrine to allow policyholders to recover for hurricane-related losses where their evidence showed that wind was the proximate cause of the damage, even if flooding contributed to the loss. To attempt to defend against the claim, insurers must counter the insured's evidence with evidence tending to prove that the proximate and efficient cause was one that falls outside of the coverage of the insurance policy.[44]

Recently decided cases, specifically in Mississippi, suggest that the federal courts will enforce the flood exclusion to the extent the damage is caused by flood, not wind and rain, but will not enforce anti-concurrent causation language where it would eliminate coverage for otherwise covered damage.[45] In addition, because insurers bear the burden of proving allocation of loss between wind/rain (covered) and flood (excluded), insurers will likely be held liable for paying all Katrina damage for which the cause of loss cannot be definitely established.[46]

Unfair Claims Practices State Laws

In addition to the application of the efficient proximate cause doctrine to uphold or not uphold coverage in favor of policyholders, most states and jurisdictions have regulations and rules on claims handling that provide certain protection to policyholders. Most states have adopted a_ version of the National Association of Insurance Commissioners (NAIC) *Model Unfair*

Claims Practices Act that governs how insurers must deal with claimants. These statutes require insurance companies to handle claims with good faith and fair dealing. Insurers, for example, must pay claims according to standards of practice, which is within 30 days after receipt of a "Proof of Loss"—i.e., a legal document that states the amount the policyholder is claiming under the policy. In the course of insurance litigation, the interpretation of specific insurance statutory and regulatory provisions comes into play. Lawsuits frequently arise alleging insurer violation of specific provisions (e.g., unfair claim settlement practices, delay in settling claims, etc.).

SUMMARY OF KATRINA LITIGATION

Katrina spawned hundreds of lawsuits against insurance companies,[47] most challenging insurers' reliance on the water-damage exclusion and the anti-concurrent causation language in homeowners' policies to deny property damage claims. Among the issues is the extent to which the anti-concurrent causation language is consistent with or contrary to the settlement law in a given state. This section provides a brief, narrative summary of major legal activities related to Katrina insurance claims disputes.

"Valued Policy" Statutes and Related Litigation

Policyholders typically use the "valued policy" statutes to gain coverage in cases where both wind and water caused damage to the property. Valued policy statutes require insurers to determine the value of the property being insured at the time a policy is written and to pay that full value to the insured when there is a total loss caused by a covered peril. The insured is not required to prove the value of the damaged property. A building is considered a total loss when the necessary repair costs are more than 50% of the value of the building.

Both Louisiana and Mississippi have enacted "valued policy" statutes as follows:

> The Louisiana Valued Policy statute provides that:
>
> Under any fire insurance policy insuring inanimate, immovable property in this state, if the insurer places a valuation upon the covered property and uses such valuation for purposes of determining the premium charge to be

made under the policy, in the case of total loss the insurer shall compute and indemnify or compensate any covered loss of, or damage to, such property which occurs during the term of the policy at such valuation without deduction or offset, unless a different method is to be used in the computation of loss, in which latter case, the policy, and any application therefore, shall set forth in type of equal size, the actual method of such loss computation by the insurer.

The Mississippi Valued Policy statute provides that:

No insurance company shall knowingly issue any fire insurance policy upon property within this state for an amount which, taken with any existing insurance thereon, exceeds a fair value of the property, nor for a longer term than five years. When buildings and structures are insured against loss by fire and, situated within the state, are totally destroyed by fire, the company shall not be permitted to deny that the building or structures insured were worth at the time of the issuance of the policy the full value upon which the insurance is calculated and the measure of damages shall be the amount for which the building and structures were insured.

Mississippi has an instructive precedent regarding the water damage exclusion. Under Mississippi common law, where there is damage caused by both wind and rain (covered loss) and flood (excluded loss), the amount due under the policy will generally depend on the proximate and efficient cause of the damage (i.e., hurricane wind), even if other "non" covered causes also contributed to the loss.[48]

A Florida case found that the state's Valued policy statute did, in fact, require payment of the face amount of the wind-insurance policy because the insured property was damaged—at least in part—by a covered peril (wind).[49] The special concurrence in *Mierzwa* would have required that the "proximate cause" of the damage be the covered peril (wind) (and not merely, as the majority held, that it be *some part* of the cause of the damage), but agreed with the majority result because the concurrer found such "proximate cause."[50] The Florida statute, however, was amended after the *Mierzwa* decision to specifically allow for the pro rating of damages caused by both a covered and a non-covered peril except "if the covered perils alone would have caused the total loss."[51]

Several cases from Louisiana have been filed, presumably seeking to rely on *Mierzwa*, attempting to get insurers to cover their damages—notwithstanding that the Louisiana valued policy statute is directed specifically at fire insurance policies.

Concluding Observations

Several concluding observations could be made.

- One major problem that has been identified is that the NFIP flood coverage and the private market wind coverage are provided under separate coverage forms, many times by separate insurers and often through separate distribution mechanisms. Congress might choose to focus on the identified problem: flood and wind coverages do not intersect. The NFIP's WYO program works today because the flood policy is typically sold by the same personal lines agent and through the same personal lines insurer that offer the basic property policy. The challenge for policymakers and insurers is to develop better coordination between flood and wind coverage.
- A major problem with the current system of flood risk mapping is the incorporation of the latest information on risk. When there is evidence that risk levels are rising or that risk was previously underestimated, it can be difficult to get the appropriate adjustments approved. As an illustration, climatologists have observed that the nation is in a period of higher hurricane activity and rising sea levels. The NFIP's coastal storm surge flood zones at any return period may extend further inland than are shown on the official FEMA flood maps. As a result, the construction of buildings at dangerously low elevations will continue to be permitted. In 2006, FEMA announced it was in the process of issuing new flood maps for the City of New Orleans and areas of Mississippi. Until such time as these maps are available, FEMA has issued Advisory Base Flood Elevations (BFEs), which direct areas "protected by levees to elevate substantially damaged homes and businesses to 3 feet above the highest adjacent existing grade on site or the current BFE on the flood insurance rate map, whichever is higher."
- NFIP has a low level of market penetration. Despite a requirement that many policyholders purchase NFIP coverage, a much lower than expected number do. Many of those that claim "wind / flood" issues appear to be attacking the private insurance policy's flood exclusion because the policyholder did not purchase NFIP coverage. Congress faces relatively low levels of participation in the NFIP.

End Notes

[1] See Lloyd Dixon, Noreen Clancy, Seth A. Seabury, "The National Flood Insurance Program's Market Penetration Rate: Estimates and Policy Implications," *Rand Corporation*, March13, 2006, located at http://www.rand.org/pubs/ technical_reports/2006/RAND_TR300.pdf.

[2] The term "anti-concurrent causation language" refers to language that is typically inserted in an insurance policy to make it as clear and unambiguous as possible that a specific risk is not covered. Insurers use this type of language in contracts in an attempt to prevent policyholders from seeking coverage for losses they never intend to cover.

[3] Matt Brady, "U.S. Representative Taylor Seeks Probe of Insurers," *National Underwriter Online News Service*, January 12, 2007.

[4] Arthur D. Postal, "Gulf Congressmen Attack Insurers on Many Fronts," *National Underwriter Online News Service*, January 19, 2007.

[5] U.S. Government Accountability Office, *National Flood Insurance Program: Greater Transparency and Oversight of Wind and Flood Damage Determinations are Needed,* http://www.gao.gov/new.items/d0828.pdf, visited on January 30, 2008.

[6] For a brief discussion of what the McCarran-Ferguson Act does and does not cover, as well as some McCarran-related legislation in the 109th Congress, see CRS Report RL33683, *Courts Narrow McCarran-Ferguson Antitrust Exemption for "Business of Insurance": Viability of "State Action" Doctrine as an Alternative*, by Janice E. Rubin.

[7] Bill Mellander, "Payouts Hinge on the Cause of Damage," *New York Times*, August 31, 2005, p. C5.

[8] Council of Economic Advisers, *Economic Report of the President*, February 2007, p. 120.

[9] Matt Fellowes and Amy Liu, "Federal Allocations in Response to Katrina, Rita and Wilma: An Update," *The Brookings Institutions*, located at http://www.brookings.edu/metro/pubs/ 20060712_katrinafactsheet.pdf#search=%22community%20development%20block%20gra nt%20and%20katrina%20fl ood%20relief%22.

[10] See Letter from Donald B. Marron, Acting Director of Congressional Budget Office, to Honorable Judd Gregg, Chairman, Committee on the Budget, May 31, 2006, located at http://www.cbo.gov/ftpdocs/72xx/doc7233/05-31-NFIPLetterGregg.pdf.

[11] WYO insurers are private insurers who have agreed to sell and service NFIP policies, and adjust flood insurance claims under a contractual agreement with FEMA.

[12] These property owners or loans include (1) loans from federally regulated lending institutions; (2) loans that are purchased by the Federal National Mortgage Association (Fannie Mae) or the Federal Home Loan Mortgage Corporation (Freddie Mac); and (3) property owners who receive federal financial assistance for acquisition or construction purposes in SFHAs in communities that participate in the NFIP.

[13] P.L. 93-234; 87 Stat. 975.

[14] P.L. 103-325; 108 Stat. 2255.

[15] See Lloyd Dixon, Noreen Clancy, Seth A. Seabury, "The National Flood Insurance Program's Market Penetration Rate: Estimates and Policy Implications," *Rand Corporation*, March 13, 2006, located at http://www.rand.org/pubs/ technical_reports/2006/RAND_TR300.pdf

[16] Ibid.

[17] Howard Kunreuther, "Has the Time Come for Comprehensive Natural Disaster Insurance?" in *On Risk and Disaster: Lessons from Hurricane Katrina*, Roland J. Daniels, Donald F. Kettle, eds. (Philadelphia: University of Pennsylvania Press, 2006), p. 175.

[18] Howard Kunreuther and M. Pauly, "Rules Rather than Discretion: Lessons from Hurricane Katrina," *Journal of Risk and Uncertainty*, 2006, vol. 33, pp. 101-116.

[19] Howard Kunreuther and M. Pauly, "Neglecting Disaster: Why Don't People Insure Against Large Losses?" *Journal of Risk and Uncertainty*, 2004, vol. 28, pp. 5-21.

[20] For more information on flood insurance reform see CRS Report RL34052, *The Flood Insurance Reform and Modernization Act of 2007: A Summary of Key Provisions*, by Rawle O. King.

[21] Office of Inspector General, Department of Homeland Security, "Challenges in FEMA's Flood Map Modernization Program," Report No. OIG-05-44, September 2005, located at http://oversight.house.gov/Documents/ 20051018124029-72925.pdf.

[22] Ibid.

[23] Peter Whorisky, "Risk Estimates Led to Fewer Flood Policies," *Washington Post*, October 17, 2005, p. A 1.

[24] Ibid.

[25] P.L. 79-15; 59 Stat. 33

[26] See Daniel A. Farber, "Disasters and the Law: Katrina and Beyond" (Aspen Publishers: 2006.)

[27] Adverse selection is the tendency of people who have a greater perceived probability of loss than does the average person to seek insurance.

[28] P.L. 90-448, 82 Stat 573.

[29] In order to assess a community's flood risk which is delineated on FIRMs, FEMA uses historical flood data, including the community's rainfall and river-flow, topography, wind velocity, tidal surge, flood-control measures, development, and other factors.

[30] The Insurance Services Office, Inc. (ISO) is an insurance organization that provides statistical information, actuarial analyses and consulting, policy language, and technical services to insurers.

[31] Buente v. Allstate Prop. and Cas. Ins. Co., 2006 WL 980784 (S.D. Miss. 4/12/2006).

[32] Tuepker v. State Farm Fire and Cas., 2006 WL 1442489 (S.D. Miss. 5/24/2006).

[33] Ibid., p. 4.

[34] Ibid., p. 6.

[35] The controversial issue involving the allocation of damage between wind and water is not present in the commercial insurance marketplace because flood/water damage is covered. To the extent an issue might arise, it is with respect to sublimits for damage from flood. For example, a commercial building could be insured for $200 million but with a $30 million sublimit for flood.

[36] See J. Robert Hunter, *Property/Casualty Insurance in 2007: Overpriced Insurance, Underpaid Claims, Declining Losses and Unjustified Profits*, January 8, 2007, located at http://www.centerjd.org/free/mythbusters-free/ CFA_070108.pdf.

[37] See Collins Center for Public Policy, *Issue Paper: National Flood Insurance Program*, located at http://www.fldfs.com/PressOffice/Documents/RetrieveDocument.asp?DocumentID= %7B115A82E4-01B1-44C6-874D-6950E134524D%7D.

[38] Ibid.

[39] Causation issues may extend beyond the question of windstorm versus flood. For example, damage to buildings may be linked to pre-existing structural deficiencies or to outside forces such as vandalism. Mold in buildings may have been there before any flooding. Yet another issue is damages resulting from the levee break. A key question is: What is the chain of causation? The breach of a levees built by government authorities would presumably involve two entirely independent causes that combine to result in loss or damage, but neither set the other in motion. In this case, "coverage under a policy is equally available to an insured whenever an insured risk constitutes simply a concurrent proximate cause of the injuries." Policyholders have been able to argue successfully that while a policy might exclude flooding, it did not exclude the independent concurrent cause of negligence in design or maintenance of levees. In other words, because the loss resulted from the occurrence of an excluded hazard *and* a covered hazard, it should be covered.

[40] Seth A. Tucker and Ann-Kelley Kemper, "Hurricane Katrina Insurance Coverage Issues," *Covington & Burling*, October4, 2005, located at http://www.cov.com/files/Publication/ 0a096d9d-4741-4cd3-bee7-7359422c2a3a/ Presentation/PublicationAttachment/61063844-2886-44d8-bac4-7f5c3bbecafe/oid27267.pdf.

[41] See Doug Simpson's weblog, *Unintended Consequences: Flood Insurance and Exclusions, Proximate and Concurrent Causation*, located at *http://www.dougsimpson.c* om/blog/archives/000464.html.

[42] For expert commentary on causation in insurance contract interpretation, see *The Enigma of Causation in Insurance Contract Interpretation*, Kenneth S. Wollner, http://www.irmi.com/ irmicom/expert/articles/2003/wollner01.aspx.

[43] Western Assurance Co. v. Hann, 78 So. 232 (Ala. 1971); Glens Falls Ins. Co. of Glens Falls, N.Y. v. Linwood Elevator, 130 So. 2d 262, 270 (Miss. 1961); Evans Plantation, Inc. V. Yorkshire Ins. Co, 58 So. 2d 797, 798 (Miss. 1952); Roach-Strayhan-Holland Post No. 20, American Legion Club, Inc. v. Continental Ins. Co. of N.Y., 112 So. 2d 680 (La. 1959).

[44] See, e.g., Broussard v. State Farm Fire and Casualty Company, Civil Action No. 1:06cv6-LTS-RHW (S.D. Miss. 1/11/2007) (on cross-motions for judgment as a matter of law).

[45] E.g., Leonard v. Nationwide Mutual Ins. Co., 438 F. Supp. 2d 684 (S.D. Miss. 2006).

[46] *Broussard, supra.*

[47] Daniel Hays and Susanne Sclafane, "Mississippi Negotiating Katrina Settlements: Deal With State Farm Reportedly Near," *National Underwriter: Property & Casualty*, January 15, 2007.

[48] See Grace v. Lititz Mutual Insurance Co. 257 So. 2d 217 (Miss. 1972).

[49] Mierzwa v. Florida Windstorm Underwriting Association, 877 So.2d 774 (Fla. App. 2004).

[50] 877 So. 2d at 781-2.

[51] *See* West's F.S.A. § 627.702(1)(b), effective 6/1/2005.

In: National and Mandatory Flood Insurance ISBN: 978-1-61209-126-6
Editors: A. Muñoz and M. Phillips

Chapter 5

FLOOD INSURANCE: FEMA'S RATE-SETTING PROCESS WARRANTS ATTENTION

United States Government Accountability Office

WHY GAO DID THIS STUDY

Questions about the financial status of the National Flood Insurance Program (NFIP) have increased since the 2005 hurricanes, which left the program with an unprecedented $17.4 billion deficit—a debt that resulted in GAO placing NFIP on its high-risk list in March 2006. Among the concerns are the subsidized rates NFIP must provide for about 25 percent of the policies, mostly for older buildings in high-risk flood zones. And although fully risk-based rates are supposed to reflect actual flood risk, concerns have been raised that they do not. This chapter evaluates (1) the Federal Emergency Management Agency's (FEMA) process for setting full-risk rates to determine whether it produces rates that accurately reflect the risk of flooding and (2) the process that FEMA uses to set subsidized rates and their effect on the financial condition of NFIP. To do this work, GAO evaluated the NFIP rate model, examined data from FEMA, surveyed relevant literature, and interviewed other relevant agencies and risk-modeling firms.

What GAO Recommends

GAO recommends that FEMA (1) ensure that its rate-setting methods result in rates that accurately reflect flood risks and (2) collect data to analyze the impact of newly created grandfathered properties on the NFIP. FEMA generally concurred with both recommendations but expressed two reservations with our recommendation regarding rate setting.

What GAO Found

FEMA's method for setting its full-risk rates may not ensure that the rates accurately reflect the actual risk of flood damage. The NFIP model combines estimated flood risk with expected flood damage, but a number of factors may affect the accuracy of the rates the model generates. First, some data inputs are outdated or inaccurate. FEMA relies on flood probabilities from the 1980s and damage estimates that do not fully reflect recent NFIP damage experience. Moreover, while FEMA has made updating its flood maps a priority, most of the maps used in rate setting have not yet been updated. Second, FEMA does not require all properties remapped into higher-risk areas to pay rates based on the new designation. This policy, known as grandfathering, erodes NFIP's ability to charge rates that reflect the risk of flooding. The policy is intended to increase participation, but FEMA does not track the number of grandfathered properties and cannot determine their financial impact on the program. Third, FEMA uses a nationwide rating system that combines flood zones across many geographic areas, so individual policies do not always reflect topographical features that affect flood risk. In fact, some patterns in historical claims and premium data suggest that NFIP's full-risk rates may not always reflect actual flood risk. Collectively, these factors increase the risk that premiums collected on full-risk policies may be insufficient to cover future losses, adding to concerns about NFIP's financial stability.

FEMA's rate-setting process for subsidized properties depends in part on the accuracy of the full-risk rates, raising concerns about how these rates are calculated as well. To set subsidized rates, FEMA first subtracts the total amount it expects to collect in full-risk premiums from the average historical loss year—that is, the minimum (target) amount that the program needs to collect from all premiums to cover at least average annual losses, as determined by historical data. The remainder becomes the aggregate target amount the program must collect in subsidized premiums. To set individual subsidized rates, FEMA officials then consider their knowledge of flood risk, previous rate increases for various locations, and statutory limits on increases. The resulting subsidized premiums continue to be a financial strain on the NFIP and contribute to its ongoing financial instability. Evidence suggests that flooding is likely to become more severe in the future, resulting in increased risk exposure, the potential for more catastrophic losses, and ongoing financial instability for the program. Currently, the annual amount that NFIP collects in both full-risk and subsidized premiums is not enough to cover its operating costs, claim losses, and principal and interest payments to the Department of the Treasury, thereby exposing the federal government and ultimately taxpayers to ever-greater financial risks, especially in years of catastrophic flooding.

ABBREVIATIONS

BFE	base flood elevation
CBO	Congressional Budget Office
CRS	Congressional Research Service
DELV	damage by elevation
DHS	Department of Homeland Security
FEMA	Federal Emergency Management Agency
FIRM	Flood Insurance Rate Map
GAAP	Generally Accepted Accounting Principles
GDP	gross domestic product
NFIP	National Flood Insurance Program
PELV	probability of elevation
SFHA	Special Flood Hazard Area

October 31, 2008

The Honorable Richard C. Shelby
Ranking Member
Committee on Banking, Housing, and Urban Affairs
United States Senate

Dear Senator Shelby:

As of June 2008, the National Flood Insurance Program (NFIP) owed approximately $17.4 billion to the U.S. Treasury, primarily as a result of loans that the program received to pay claims resulting from the 2005 hurricane season. According to the Federal Emergency Management Agency (FEMA) of the Department of Homeland Security (DHS), which administers the program, this debt is greater than the sum of all previous losses since the program's inception in 1968. Until 2004, NFIP was able to cover most of its losses with the premiums it collected and occasional loans from the Treasury that were either repaid or retired by Congress. However, after the 2005 hurricanes—primarily Hurricane Katrina—the program borrowed $16.8 billion from the Treasury to cover the enormous number of claims. As a result, in part because of the level of indebtedness, we placed NFIP on our high-risk list in March 2006.[1]

As a result of this unprecedented deficit, questions have been raised about the fiscal sustainability of the flood insurance program, particularly given the potential for similar natural disasters in the future. Congress and others have raised questions about the scope of the information and quality of the data on which the program relies to set premium rates and the accuracy of the maps NFIP uses to assess the risk of flooding.[2] FEMA's process for setting premium rates determines how much policyholders will pay for their flood insurance policies and thus the income available to FEMA for losses and expenses. By statute, NFIP was not designed to be actuarially sound. Premium rates for most properties—around 75 percent—are intended to fully reflect the risk of flooding, but the remaining 25 percent are subsidized, as mandated by statute. While these subsidized premiums do not contribute sufficient revenues to cover potential losses, according to FEMA officials, they promote participation in the program, an important program goal. But as a result, the program does not collect sufficient premium income to build capital to cover flood losses.

In response to the questions that have been raised about NFIP's financial condition, this chapter evaluates (1) FEMA's process for setting full-risk premiums to determine whether it produces rates that accurately reflect the risk of flooding and (2) the process that FEMA uses to set subsidized rates and their financial impact on NFIP.

To address these objectives, we obtained and reviewed FEMA's flood risk model and related methods for assessing risk and setting premium rates for policyholders. We discussed FEMA's method for setting rates with officials from FEMA, the National Oceanic and Atmospheric Administration, U.S.

Army Corps of Engineers (the Corps), and the U.S. Geological Survey. We also met with risk-modeling firms, academics, and the American Academy of Actuaries and reviewed studies of flood risk and flood insurance, including reviews from the Congressional Research Service (CRS) and the Congressional Budget Office (CBO). We also analyzed premiums received and losses paid by NFIP for the period from 1978 to 2007. We assessed the reliability of these data, and found them to be reliable for the purposes of this chapter. In addition, we obtained and reviewed information on FEMA's current and past borrowings and repayments. We also analyzed FEMA's premiums and claims data to determine the number of high-loss years on a state-by-state basis in order to assess each state's financial impact on NFIP. In order to conduct the state loss analysis, we reviewed the claims and premium data from NFIP's BureauNet database.[3] Appendix I provides additional details about our scope and methodology.

We conducted this performance audit from December 2007 to September 2008 in accordance with generally accepted government auditing standards. Those standards require that we plan and perform the audit to obtain sufficient, appropriate evidence to provide a reasonable basis for our findings and conclusions based on our audit objectives. The evidence we obtained provides a reasonable basis for our findings and conclusions based on our audit objectives.

Results in Brief

FEMA's method for setting full-risk rates may not ensure that the rates accurately reflect the actual risk of flood damage.[4] FEMA's model for setting these rates incorporates data on flood risks generated by a hydrologic model that is based on largely the same principles as hazard risk models used by private insurers and other federal agencies.[5] More specifically, FEMA generates rates for flood insurance according to estimates of flood risk and expected flood damage. However, a number of factors may affect the accuracy of rates generated by the process. First, the data that FEMA uses to define flood probabilities are outdated or inaccurate. For example, some of the data used to estimate the probability of flooding have not been updated since the 1980s. Similarly, the claims data used as inputs to the model may be inaccurate because of incomplete claims records and missing data. Further, the maps FEMA uses to set premium rates remain substantially out of date despite recent modernization efforts. In addition, an NFIP policy decision allows certain properties remapped into riskier flood zones to keep their previous lower rates, which, like subsidized rates, do not reflect the actual risk of flooding to the properties and do not generate sufficient premiums to cover expected losses.[6] Moreover, FEMA does not collect data on these properties—known as grandfathered properties—or measure their financial impact on the program and does not know how many of these properties exist, their exact location, or how much they generate in losses. FEMA's rate-setting process also does not fully take into account ongoing and planned development, long-term trends in erosion, or the effects of global climate change, although private sector models are incorporating some of these factors. Finally, FEMA sets flood insurance rates on a nationwide basis, combining and averaging many topographic factors that are relevant to flood risk, so that these factors are not specifically accounted for in setting rates for individual properties. Moreover, some patterns in historical claims and premium data suggest that NFIP's rates may not accurately reflect differences in flood risk. Collectively, these factors increase the risk that full-risk premiums may be insufficient to cover future losses, adding to concerns about NFIP's financial stability.

FEMA's rate-setting process for subsidized properties depends in part on the accuracy of the full-risk rates, raising concerns about how subsidized rates are calculated as well. To determine subsidized rates, FEMA first subtracts the total amount that it expects to collect on full-risk rate premiums from the average historical loss year target. This target is the minimum amount of premiums the program needs to collect to cover at least average annual losses, as determined by historical loss data. The amount remaining from this calculation is the aggregate target amount of subsidized premiums that the program needs to collect. To set individual subsidized rates, FEMA officials then consider their knowledge of flood risks, previous rate increases for various areas, and statutory limits on increases. According to FEMA documents, the method for determining the average historical loss year target was changed in 2006 because fully incorporating the 2005 loss year, with its catastrophic losses, would have resulted in substantial increases in subsidized rates. Currently, the annual amount that NFIP collects in both full-risk and subsidized premiums is not enough to cover its operating costs, claim losses, and principal and interest payments to the Department of the Treasury. Evidence suggests that flooding is likely to become more severe in the future, resulting in increased risk exposure, the potential for more catastrophic losses, and ongoing financial instability for the program. Without changes to its current rate-setting processes, NFIP premiums will be unlikely to be able to cover the program's claims, expenses, and debt, exposing the federal government and ultimately taxpayers to ever-greater financial risks, especially in years of catastrophic flooding.

This chapter makes two recommendations aimed at helping improve NFIP's rate-setting process. First, we recommend that FEMA take steps to ensure that its rate-setting methods and data used to set rates result in full-risk premiums rates that accurately reflect the risk of losses from flooding. Second, we recommend that FEMA collect information on the location, number, and losses associated with existing and newly created grandfathered properties and analyze the financial impact of these properties on the program.

We provided the Secretary of Homeland Security with a draft of this chapter for review and comment. On October 14, 2008, FEMA provided written comments on a draft of this chapter (see appendix III). FEMA generally concurred with both of the report's recommendations but had two reservations about our recommendation to ensure that FEMA's rate-setting methods result in full-risk rates that accurately reflect the risk of losses from flooding. FEMA also took exception to some of our analyses and characterizations, which it believes overstate the potential effect of different factors on the accuracy of the rate-setting process. While we acknowledge the complexity of FEMA's rate-setting process, the issues we have identified raise questions about the accuracy of the resulting premium rates and highlights areas that warrant additional analysis by FEMA. FEMA's comments are summarized near the end of this chapter, and FEMA's letter is reprinted in appendix III. FEMA also provided us with technical comments, which we incorporated as appropriate.

BACKGROUND

NFIP is a federal program created by the National Flood Insurance Act of 1968 that enables property owners in participating communities to purchase insurance protection against losses from flooding. This program is administered by FEMA. Participation in NFIP is based on an agreement between local communities and the federal government. The federal government makes flood insurance available to any community that adopts and enforces a floodplain management ordinance to reduce future flood risks to new construction in areas known as Special Flood Hazard Areas (SFHA).[7] Property owners located in the SFHA with mortgages from federally regulated lenders are required to purchase and maintain flood insurance policies. In these areas, new construction and substantial improvements must conform to NFIP's building standards.[8] For example, the lowest floor of a structure must be elevated to or above the base flood elevation (BFE)—the level at which there is a 1 percent chance of flooding in a given year.[9]

NFIP offers two types of flood insurance premiums: subsidized and full risk. The National Flood Insurance Act of 1968 requires that NFIP offer subsidized premiums to owners of certain properties. These subsidized rates are not based on flood risk and, according to FEMA, represent only about 35 to 40 percent of the full flood risk. Subsidized properties account for about 25 percent of all NFIP policies, while those with full-risk premiums account for the remaining 75 percent. The type of policy and the subsequent rate a policyholder pays depend on several property characteristics—for example, whether the structure was built after or prior to the development of the community's Flood Insurance Rate Map (FIRM) and where the structure is located relative to the floodplain. NFIP studies and maps flood risks, assigning flood zone designations based on the risk level for flooding. For our purposes, in this chapter we generally refer to risk levels as moderate- to low-risk, high-risk, high-risk coastal, and undetermined risk.[10] Potential policyholders can purchase both building and contents flood insurance for residential and commercial properties (table 1).[11]

Congress mandated the use of subsidized premiums to encourage communities to join the program and mitigate concerns that charging rates that fully and accurately reflected flood risk would be a burden to some property owners. The Flood Disaster Protection Act of 1973 made the purchase of flood insurance mandatory for the protection of properties within SFHAs that are secured by mortgages from federally regulated lenders, thus expanding the use of subsidized premiums. In addition, NFIP was authorized to begin charging full-risk premiums for all construction built after 1974 or the date of the community's initial FIRM. According to FEMA, Congress made these changes to encourage further participation in NFIP through low premiums. More recently, legislation has been introduced that would limit NFIP subsidies aimed at improving the financial stability of the program.[12]

Pre-FIRM structures generally are more prone to flood damage (that is, riskier) than structures built later because they were not constructed according to the program's building standards. Owners of post-FIRM structures generally are not eligible to receive subsidized rates. Largely because subsidized properties tend to be riskier than properties insured at full-risk premiums, in 2007, the average annual premium for a subsidized policy was about $869, while the average annual premium for a full-risk policy was about $378.[13] Flood insurance rates are calculated for each flood zone. However, as shown in table 2, flood insurance rates also depend on flood zone.

Table 1. Amounts of NFIP Insurance Available, as of May 1, 2008

Type of coverage	Emergency program	Regular program		
		Basic limit	Additional limit	Total limit
Building coverage				
Single-family dwelling	$35,000	$50,000	$200,000	**$250,000**
Two- to-four-family dwelling	35,000	50,000	200,000	**250,000**
Other residential	100,000	150,000	100,000	**250,000**
Nonresidential	100,000	150,000	350,000	**500,000**
Contents coverage				
Residential	10,000	20,000	80,000	**100,000**
Nonresidential	$100,000	$130,000	$370,000	**$500,000**

Source: NFIP rate manual.

Note: Alaska, Hawaii, Guam and the U.S. Virgin Islands have different amounts of coverage for the first and second layers of coverage; however, their total limit is also $250,000. The Emergency Flood Insurance Program is intended as a program to provide a first layer amount of insurance on all insurable structures before the effective date of the initial FIRM.

Table 2. Average Premium per Policy in Force by Flood Zone, 1997-2006

(In constant 2006 dollars)				
Calendar year	**High-risk**	**High-risk coastal**	**Moderate- to low-risk**	**Undetermined risk level**
1997	$521	$1,039	$377	$794
1998	538	1,041	384	814
1999	525	1,053	380	824
2000	497	1,049	363	788
2001	482	1,059	350	766
2002	472	1,118	343	775
2003	478	1,232	349	824
2004	492	1,343	344	842
2005	502	1,398	340	912
2006	$521	$1,463	$336	$980

Source: GAO analysis of NFIP data.

The insurance operations of NFIP differ from those of most private insurers in a number of ways. First, unlike private insurers that can reject applicants with properties whose potential losses would not be offset by premiums, NFIP is required to accept virtually all applications for insurance. Therefore, NFIP is less able to offset the effects of adverse selection—that is, the phenomenon that those who are most likely to purchase insurance are also most likely to experience losses.[14] Adverse selection may lead to a concentration of policyholders in the riskiest areas; the problem is compounded by the fact that those at greatest risk are required to purchase NFIP insurance if they have a mortgage from a federally insured lender.

Second, NFIP's ability to adjust premiums is limited by statute. While most states regulate premium prices, they tend to allow private insurers considerable flexibility in their ability to set prices. Third, NFIP assumes all the risks for the policies it sells. Private insurers typically retain only part of the risk that they accept from policyholders, ceding a portion of the risk to reinsurers.[15] This mechanism is particularly important in the case of insurance for catastrophic events, because the availability of reinsurance allows an insurer to limit the possibility that it will experience losses beyond its ability to pay.

Finally, NFIP is not authorized to charge premiums that are sufficient to build the capital that most private insurers have to offset losses or purchase reinsurance in the private global market. For example, private insurers have a capital surplus that they use to pay expected claims. In contrast, NFIP operates on a cash flow basis, backed by borrowing authority from the U.S. Treasury. As a result, NFIP does not follow all of the traditional accounting practices that private insurers use—for example, NFIP reports using only Generally Accepted Accounting Principles (GAAP) accounting, which is an ongoing operations accounting basis, while private insurers must report both GAAP and statutory accounting basis.[16]

FEMA's Method of Setting Full-Risk Premiums May Not Ensure That Rates Accurately Reflect Risk

FEMA uses a rate model to generate prices for flood insurance according to flood risk and expected flood damage. However, we found that in some cases these full-risk premiums may not accurately reflect actual risk because of limitations in the data used as inputs for the model and the effects of certain policy decisions. For instance:

- Some data FEMA used in rate setting are outdated or inaccurate, including data on flood probabilities, damage estimates, and flood maps.
- FEMA allows some properties that were remapped into riskier flood zones to keep their previous lower rates.
- FEMA's rate-setting process does not fully take into account ongoing and planned development, long-term trends in erosion, and effects of global climate change.
- FEMA sets rates on a nationwide basis, combining and averaging across many geographically diverse areas.[17]

Furthermore, our analysis of the difference between claims payments and premiums collected for all 50 states and the District of Columbia suggests that NFIP's pricing has not accurately reflected differences in flood risk. Collectively, these factors increase the risk that premiums collected on full-risk rates do not accurately reflect the risks of flooding and therefore may not be sufficient to cover future losses.

FEMA's Rate-Setting Process Uses a Model That Is Based on Flood Risk and Expected Flood Damage

According to FEMA, rates that are based on the probability of a given level of flooding, damage estimates based on that level of flooding, and acepted actuarial principles are considered to be "full risk."[18] To set rates for flood insurance that accurately reflect risk, information about the differential risk of flooding is key, with greater flood risks resulting in higher rates. Rates also vary depending on how much insurance is purchased. As claims are more likely to be made against the first several thousand dollars of coverage than against much higher levels of coverage (that is, smaller dollar-value losses are generally expected to occur more frequently than larger ones and thus pose a greater risk), rates per $100 of insurance coverage are lower for higher levels of coverage.[19]

FEMA uses a model to set rates for flood insurance for post-FIRM construction within the 1 percent, or 100-year, floodplain according to flood risk and expected resulting flood damage.[20] This method of estimating flood damage is based on the hydrologic model described in a 1966 report by the Department of Housing and Urban Development, which was based on studies conducted in the 1960s and developed and used by the Corps for a number of years.[21] While the Corps has revised its model for estimating flood damage, it still makes use of the hydrologic model to estimate flood damage.

In the high-risk and high-risk coastal zones, the model combines estimates of the frequency of flooding with estimates of the magnitude of damage caused by flooding, producing "pure premium" costs intended to cover the actual flood losses. FEMA uses such inputs as the elevation of the lowest floor of the building, the type of building, the number of floors, the presence of a basement, claims data, and mapping information to generate the estimates. This pure premium amount is then adjusted to capture certain program costs, compensate for underinsurance by policyholders, and reflect the fact that the program has a deductible.[22] For the moderate- to low-risk and other full-risk premium zones, rates have been developed based on actuarial and engineering judgments, using the rates generated by the model and the historical experience of the high-risk zones as benchmarks.[23]

While other entities employing flood models may use more sophisticated computer modeling techniques, the NFIP rate model is based largely on the same principles. In 2000, FEMA completed a feasibility study on using private market reinsurance to cover a portion of its flood risk that required modeling the frequency and size of catastrophic flood events, and determined that the results of the study were not inconsistent with the results of NFIP's rating structure. For other lines of catastrophe insurance, private insurers rely heavily on computer models of simulated damage over many possible events to price their products.[24] Like NFIP, other federal agencies and private insurers involved in flood modeling also rely on flood maps and data on the likelihood of flooding and damages. According to FEMA, it has contracted for actuarial services with an external consultant to assess the current state of hazard modeling and the possible applicability of those models to NFIP.

Some Key Data Elements Used in the Rate-Setting Model Are Outdated or Based on Erroneous Information

Questions remain about the age and quality of the underlying data FEMA uses in its model to calculate full-risk premiums. The NFIP model for setting full-risk premium rates relies on flood probability estimates and expected damage data, which rely in part on outdated or potentially inaccurate information, including outdated FIRMs. As discussed more fully below, flood probability estimates have not been updated since the 1970s and 1980s, most FIRMs are out of date despite FEMA's recent modernization efforts, and the claims data used to calculate full-risk premiums may be inaccurate. As a result, the premium rates set by NFIP may not fully reflect the risk of loss due to flooding.

Data Used to Determine Flood Probabilities Have Not Been Updated since the 1970s and 1980s

FEMA's estimates of probabilities that floods of different severities (relative to the BFE) will occur in a given year, or "probability of elevation" (PELV) values, were generated in the 1970s. Within any zone, the risk that floodwaters will reach the BFE in any year is 1 percent, but across zones the likelihood that floodwaters will reach a foot above or below that level varies. PELV tables provide detailed information, by zone, about the frequency with which floods of different elevations are expected to occur. These data were generated using detailed engineering studies, available flood data, simulations, and professional judgment and were established for each flood zone to meet generally accepted scientific parameters and legal considerations of the time. FEMA later concluded that flood probabilities were likely underestimated in some cases because of the short flood histories used in some of the studies. As a result, according to FEMA officials, some of the original PELV values were modified in the early 1980s to account for this statistical bias. They have not been revisited or updated since that time.

FEMA currently uses both the original and modified PELV values in the rate-setting process. The original PELV values contribute 80 percent to the ultimate results and the modified values 20 percent, reflecting weights set out by policies from the early 1980s, according to FEMA officials. Flood risk experts have suggested that flood probabilities (and thus flood insurance rates) are likely to change as land use (such as urban or suburban development), infrastructure (such as new bridges and culverts), and weather patterns change. FEMA could capture such changes by updating its flood probability data but has not done so.

FEMA officials also acknowledged that the weighting for the original and modified PELV values was likely out of date but said that other competing priorities, including supporting post-Katrina-related activities and other studies had been given priority.[25] Moreover, a FEMA official noted that the weighting might introduce a degree of "conservatism" to the rate-setting process because it would lead to higher rather than lower premium rates.[26] Further, according to the officials, the geographic mix of NFIP policies had become more concentrated in Florida and other communities where the PELV values were more accurate. Nevertheless, FEMA has not updated the PELV data since the 1980s or updated the weighting of the original and modified PELV data. As a result, the accuracy of the flood probability estimates and the probability of elevation values are uncertain, and we could not determine whether the rates based on such data were accurate. Moreover, FEMA was not able to provide any analysis that it had done to determine that the current weighting remained appropriate or that the probabilities had not changed in over 30 years.

The Claims Data Used in the Model May Be Inaccurate

In addition, some claims data—which are updated on a periodic basis—may suffer from errors and thus misinform damage estimates and, in turn, the rates generated by the model. FEMA relies on estimates of the percentage of the value of a structure that is expected to be damaged when a flood occurs, or the "damage by elevation" (DELV) values. DELV information is measured in 1-foot increments of the flood level within the structure and is expressed as the expected percentage of the property's value that will be damaged by a flood of that elevation.[27] As with the PELV data, information used in establishing DELV values was obtained primarily from engineering studies. In 1973, data for DELVs were selected on the basis of studies done by the Corps and available flood claims at that time. Currently, FEMA modifies the Army Corps DELV values based on its NFIP claims experience. When FEMA determines that its own loss data are "credible," it uses these data rather than the original data generated by the Corps.[28] However, FEMA also currently uses updated Corps damage data to supplement NFIP claims data where it lacks sufficient credible loss data. According to a FEMA official, for the most common type of property insured by NFIP, the claims process has become fully credible for a wide range of water depths in the structure.

However, evidence suggests that there are inaccuracies in the actual claims data used to update the DELV values. An external study noted some internal control problems with NFIP's claims database.[29] For instance, claims records were often incomplete because the claims data had been collected in the field by local adjustors for purposes of processing claims. As a result, many records did not indicate BFE or depth of flooding, clearly differentiate between wind and water losses, or capture losses above the insurance limit when damage exceeded coverage limits. In addition, Corps officials told us that they had reviewed FEMA's claims between 1998 and 2000 databases and found the data to be unreliable for their purposes. For example, according to the Corps, in some cases the claims data indicated flood damage, but flood height data were missing. FEMA's database recorded these missing height data as a flood height of zero. Our analysis of NFIP claims paid between 1978 and 2007 further supports what the Corps told us. We found an increasing percentage of claims with "0" water depth until they leveled off at between 44 and 49 percent from 1998 until 2004. In 2005 when the Gulf Coast hurricanes occurred, this percentage dropped to about 13 percent, but has risen above 22 percent in the more recent years. Thus, an erroneous data combination of positive flood damage and zero flood height was being used to develop damage curves. As a result, the Corps began to collect its own damage data, which FEMA now uses to supplement its own data.

While FEMA has acknowledged that some problems exist, it believes that these types of errors relate primarily to the most severe flooding events, which have a lower probability of occurring, involve greater water depths, and would contribute only marginally to insurance rates. FEMA officials said that they had reviewed the possible impact of such data errors and did not consider them to be significant because they believed that the zero-elevation water depth errors would overstate the amount of damage from zero amount of water in a property.[30] However, this analysis is incomplete because it does not evaluate the impact of omitting these damage amounts from the actual flood depth levels. As a result, FEMA may be unable to fully assess the overall impact of these errors or omissions on its full-risk rates, creating a risk that these premiums may not accurately reflect the actual risk of flood loss.

Maps That Provide Information for Base Flood Elevations Remain Substantially out of Date despite Modernization Efforts

FIRMs provide the information that determines BFEs, a key input in the rate-setting model. FEMA formally undertook map modernization efforts in fiscal year 2003. According to FEMA, the agency undertook map modernization for several reasons:

- Flood hazard conditions are dynamic, and many NFIP maps may not reflect recent development and/or natural changes in the environment.
- Updated NFIP maps can take advantage of revised data and improved technologies for identifying flood hazards.
- Up-to-date maps support a flood insurance program that is more closely aligned with actual risk, encourages wise community-based floodplain management, and improves citizens' flood hazard awareness.

- Local communities and various stakeholders want more timely updates of flood maps and easier access to the flood hazard data used to create the maps.

In 2005, FEMA adjusted its goals and currently expects to provide updated flood boundaries for 75 percent of stream miles reflected on FEMA's issued maps and 0.30 percent of those mapped stream miles will be based on new or updated engineering studies by the end of the program in 2010. FEMA also revised its goal of having digitized maps that covered 100 percent of the population to having digitized maps for 92 percent of the population so that it could better focus its efforts and thus improve map quality. FEMA undertook these changes in response to concerns expressed by Congress and DHS's Inspector General's office and in response to our prior work on this issue.[31] FEMA officials stated that changes in land use and structural development that had occurred over time would be captured when FEMA updated the FIRMs, each of which is required to be reassessed every 5 years.[32]

According to FEMA, as of May 2008, approximately 4 percent of U.S. counties had maps that accurately reflect the current risk of flooding (fully updated) and were newly digitized and 2 percent had old maps that may or may not accurately reflect the actual risk of flooding but were newly digitized. For the remaining 94 percent of U.S. counties, the maps were a combination of new and old mapping data that were in production or have not yet begun the process. According to FEMA officials, although maps for 94 percent of U.S. counties had not been fully updated or newly digitized, all counties had received a partial update to their flood hazard information and more than a third had received updates that exceeded one of FEMA's national map quality targets.[33] FEMA further stated that in March 2008, approximately 68 percent of the nation's population had received a map that met, exceeded or at least approached map quality targets of map modernization. An additional 27 percent of the population has received a preliminary map. FEMA informed us that it anticipates that 92 percent of the nation's population will have a modernized map by 2010.

However, although FEMA has been working to update FIRMs and improve their quality, a significant portion of the maps reflect data at least 15 years old, which may or may not accurately reflect actual risk of flooding. As of April 2008, 50 percent of the nation's approximately 105,700 flood maps were at least 15 years old, 58 percent were more than 10 years old, and 70 percent were at least 5 years old. To the extent that these older maps are inaccurate and the risk of flooding has changed, reliance on these older maps could lead to inaccurate flood risk assessments, which in turn could lead to inaccurate premium rates.

FEMA Does Not Track the Number or Location of Remapped Grandfathered Properties That Pay Less than Full-Risk Premiums

FEMA made a policy decision to grandfather into the program certain properties, that is, it allowed properties that have been remapped into riskier flood zones to keep their previous lower rates. FEMA is in the process of updating FIRMs through its Map Modernization program, but these new maps may not lead to more accurate pricing due to this policy decision, which was based primarily on concerns about the affordability of the resulting rates.[34] FEMA documents state that properties are grandfathered in order to recognize policyholders who have complied with their original FIRM, have remained loyal NFIP customers, or both. In general, two categories of buildings may be grandfathered into the program: (1) those built in compliance with the FIRM that was in effect at the time of construction and (2) those built before a FIRM was in effect or that were not in compliance at the time of construction.[35] For those buildings in compliance at the time of construction, property owners need to provide documentation of the date of the original FIRM and the property's flood zone, BFE, and other map-related information. Properties that were not in compliance generally can be grandfathered if they have had continuous flood insurance and if the building has not been altered in certain ways. FEMA officials told us that while grandfathering can work as a disincentive for sound floodplain management, the decision to grandfather rates was based on consideration of (1) equity, (2) ease of administration, and (3) goals of promoting flood plain management.[36]

While FEMA does not consider the premiums on these properties to be subsidized because they are based on the average risk for the whole class to which they had been assigned previously, they share two characteristics with subsidized rates. First, rates based on new FIRMs should more accurately reflect flood risk, but grandfathered properties will not be charged those rates. Second, the grandfathered status of a property continues indefinitely, even when the property is sold. FEMA officials acknowledged that property owners that obtain grandfathered rates for their homes are being cross-subsidized by other policyholders in the same zone that are paying higher rates.[37] For example, under grandfathering, repetitive loss properties remapped into a higher-risk zone instead would pay a rate generally charged to lower-risk properties.

While grandfathered rates are used to keep existing policyholders, FEMA has not taken steps to measure the impact of these rates on the program's financial condition. FEMA officials said that they currently had limited data on new or existing grandfathered properties and are just beginning to explore ways to track these properties. For example, they had not tracked the number of grandfathered properties or calculated how much lower grandfathered premiums are than the actual rates. As a result, they did not know the effect of grandfathered properties on the program's total premium collection and the extent to which these rates deviate from fully risk-based rates. Without this information, FEMA's ability to address the financial impact of such properties on NFIP's financial health is limited. FEMA officials acknowledged the importance of tracking information related to grandfathered properties and told us they plan to start a tracking process in May 2009.[38] However, they said that this process will not capture the inventory of existing grandfathered properties.

FEMA Does Not Consider Risk Factors Such as Erosion and Climate Change when Setting Flood Insurance Rates

Some experts with whom we spoke have suggested that incorporating ongoing and planned development, erosion trends, and climate change into flood risk modeling would more fully capture longer-term flood risk exposure, but FEMA does not take these variables into account. FEMA's present policy is to map SFHAs based on current development conditions. However, as floodplains are developed and more ground surfaces are paved or made impervious (nonabsorbent), the risks and expected elevations of flooding increase. As the predicted elevation of the base flood increases, SFHAs subsequently spread beyond mapped boundaries. As a result, in rapidly developing watersheds or where characteristics change significantly due to flood control projects or other natural events, some FIRMs may become outdated shortly after their completion. In addition, some properties could be constructed without proper protection from the flood hazard they may face throughout their life span, and others could be uninsured or subject to insurance rates that do not accurately reflect flood risk.

FEMA's current flood hazard mapping procedures for coastal areas incorporate storm-induced coastal erosion but not long-term erosion.[39] While shorelines, dunes, and bluffs can retreat during a single storm, long-term erosion at a shoreline is the net result of a variety of factors such as sediment losses from storms and inundation from sea level rise, averaged over several decades.[40] A 2000 study conducted for FEMA by the H. John Heinz Center estimated that over the next 60 years, losses due to the effects of coastal erosion would average $80 million annually.[41] If coastal development continues at its current pace, or if sea levels rise as some scientists have predicted, such losses could be even greater. In the absence of the authority needed to establish erosion zones, FEMA has taken action based on the results of the study, namely, a steady annual increase in rates for the high-risk coastal zone at a pace it says is commensurate with the study's projections.[42] In addition, according to FEMA officials, they formed an internal working group to determine additional actions that could be taken to implement the report's recommendations under the existing laws and regulations that govern NFIP. The working group concluded that because of the statutory limitations, implementing the recommendations would require direct congressional authorization.[43] Therefore, FEMA, which does not currently map erosion hazard areas, is unable, through its rate-setting process, to inform policyholders of the risk to their property from erosion. Consequently, in some cases flood insurance rates may send a false signal that understates the risk exposure faced by current policyholders or prospective development.

FEMA also does not incorporate the potential effects of climate change into its rate-setting considerations. Our 2007 report on climate change discussed the effects of climate change on weather-related events and, subsequently, insured and uninsured losses. We found that leading scientific bodies expect warmer temperatures to increase the frequency and severity of damaging extreme weather-related events.[44] In addition, population growth in hazard-prone areas and the resulting development and increasing real estate values have increased the exposure of federal and private insurers. In particular, heavily populated areas along the Northeast, Southeast, and Texas coasts, which are at the highest risk for major hurricanes, also have some of the highest value properties in the United States. Because of these and other factors, our report estimates that NFIP's exposure has grown substantially, quadrupling since 1980 and nearing $1 trillion.

While many private insurers are beginning to take climate change into account, FEMA has done little to develop the kind of information needed to understand the long-term exposure of NFIP to climate change for a variety of reasons. For instance, NFIP's goals are fundamentally different from those of private insurers. Specifically, private insurers stress the financial success of their business operations, but the law authorizing the federal flood insurance program promotes affordable coverage and broad participation by individuals at risk. In addition, although FEMA manages its risk within statutory guidelines, unlike private insurers, NFIP is neither required nor permitted to limit its catastrophic risk strictly within its ability to pay claims on an annual basis. One important implication of this lack of limits on managing catastrophic risk is that FEMA has little reason to develop information on NFIP's long-term exposure to the potential risk of increased low-frequency, high-severity weather events associated with climate change. NFIP's risk management processes adapt to near-term changes in weather as they affect existing data. As a result, NFIP is designed to assess and insure against current—not future—risks and currently does not have the information necessary to adjust rates for the potential impacts of events associated with climate.[45] FEMA told us that it has commissioned a study to assess the long-term exposure to climate change that will investigate changes in sea levels, intensity and frequency of hurricanes, and precipitation patterns.

FEMA's Rating System Combines and Averages Many Different Risks to Create Nationwide Rates

FEMA classifies properties according to flood risk using a single, nationwide class-rating system rather than an individual property or community-by-community rating system. That is, all properties grouped into a class—based on structure type and elevation relative to the BFE—are assumed to have the same risk.[46] Further, FEMA charges the same rate for a given class in the high-risk zone (or separately, in the high-risk coastal zone) regardless of location within the zone. Thus, two properties in the same class but located on vastly different terrain—for example, one in a shallow floodplain and the other in a steep and narrow mountain valley—are charged the same rate per $100 of insurance coverage despite the fact that they may have different expected loss.

The NFIP model can incorporate specific topographic (that is, flood zone) information in rate setting. However, according to FEMA, it was determined that more averaging could be justified, because the differences in rates across flood zones were not significant enough to warrant that level of detail. According to FEMA officials, the class-rating approach balanced the need to recognize significant differences in risk with a simplified process for determining rates that was easier for the sales force and others to use. FEMA has not revisited its class-rating approach since its inception although certain program elements have changed since that time. For example, program participation has more than doubled from just over 2 million policies to more than 5.2 million from the late 1980s to 2007 and increased numbers of properties have been constructed on SFHAs. As a result of the growth in the program, the rate classes may not accurately reflect the actual flood risk to individual properties and averaging may no longer accurately reflect differences in rates within zones.

Table 3. States Where Claims Frequently or Rarely Exceeded Premiums, 1978–2007

In constant 2007 dollars			
State	**1978-2004 premiums minus claims**	**1978-2007 premiums minus claims**	**1978-2007 Number of years that claims exceeded premiums**
Missouri	($384,344,855)	($350,344,220)	11
West Virginia	(146,896,812)	(118,874,830)	11
Mississippi	(40,584,822)	(2,498,544,520)	10
Louisiana	428,383,041	(11,777,260,456)	10
Texas	(728,796,632)	(222,265,084)	9
Alabama	(505,212,107)	(746,166,995)	9
Illinois	90,321,291	162,050,972	9
Ohio	101,547,985	100,111,514	9
New Hampshire	36,648,547	21,531,170	8
Utah	15,372,336	21,207,776	2
Wyoming	16,597,320	21,134,460	2
Nevada	70,283,808	82,293,838	2
Vermont	23,425,436	30,590,342	1
Idaho	32,991,914	42,892,136	1
Oregon	104,014,018	133,186,375	1
South Carolina	313,400,772	590,371,633	1
Florida	8,035,673,802	9,938,638,592	1
Alaska	23,003,446	27,770,628	0
New Mexico	79,909,374	97,876,034	0
Colorado	$135,763,975	$170,139,136	0

Source: GAO analysis of FEMA data.

Note: We analyzed two time periods so we could separately consider the impact of the 2005 Hurricanes Katrina, Rita, and Wilma. The numbers in parenthesis denote negative values.

Our Analysis of Historical Claims and Premium Data Raises Questions about a Potential Mismatch between Rates and Risk

We analyzed 30 years of NFIP data on claims and premiums and found patterns based on differences among states indicating that NFIP rates may not have always accurately reflected differences in flood risk.[47] As we have seen, FEMA sets premium rates that apply nationwide. Our state-by-state analysis of annual claims and premiums data dating back to 1978 showed that some states consistently had more years in which claims exceeded premiums than did other states over this period, raising questions about a potential mismatch between rates and risk.[48] It is important to note that claims equaling premiums in a given year would not indicate a break-even year, because in addition to covering expected claims in a year, a portion of premiums is also intended to cover expenses necessary to operate NFIP. For example, in the year ending May 1, 2008, NFIP projects about 53 percent of its total expenses would pay for claims, while the rest would cover other expenses such as interest on debt, loss adjustment expense, and agents' commissions. For the purposes of this chapter, we assigned the title of high-loss year to any year in which a state's claims exceeded its premiums, because in these years, these states would not have had any premium dollars left over to contribute toward administrative expenses once claims had been paid.

On an annual basis, we found that for 1978-2007, nine states had high-loss years more often than once every 4 years (table 3). Missouri and West Virginia had the most high-loss years, with 11; Alabama, Illinois, Louisiana, Mississippi, New Hampshire, Ohio, and Texas followed, with from 8 to 10 such years. Other states had very few high-loss years, and some had none. For example, Alaska, Colorado, and New Mexico had no high-loss years, while Florida, Idaho, Oregon, South Carolina, and Vermont had 1, and Nevada, Utah, and Wyoming had 2.[49] The consistency with which some states were at one extreme of the high-loss-year distribution or the other since the late 1970s suggests that NFIP's method of setting flood insurance rates on a nationwide basis may not accurately reflect differences in flood risk among states, because rates for similar properties do not vary by state.

We recognize that flooding is a highly variable event, with losses varying widely from year to year, and that even an analysis of nearly three decades of historical data could lead to unreliable conclusions about the actual flood risk faced by a given state. In addition, we note that Florida, Texas, and Louisiana are among the states with the most NFIP policies, and therefore have a more significant impact on the amount of premiums collected than other states.

Some discrepancies in high-loss years among states are to be expected and do not necessarily indicate that NFIP premium rates are mispriced. However, if some states frequently have high-loss years or rarely or never have such years, questions arise about the rate structure, because policyholders in states with frequent high-loss years are paying the same rates as policyholders with similar properties in states with fewer losses.

Additional study would be required to determine whether policyholders in some states with lower losses are paying a higher premium than is appropriate for their risk, and others paying too little. For example, our analysis did not control for differences in the type of policy purchased, such as the mix of certain property types across states and insurance coverage amounts, which could affect both premiums and claims. In addition, we did not control for differences in the mix of subsidized and full-risk policies or the impact of subsidized premiums on our results, which could also affect the results.[50] Despite these limitations, however, this analysis raises a number of questions that may warrant further study that could provide useful insights into the use of nationwide rates as well as other aspects of the program.

Collectively, these factors raise questions about FEMA's rate-setting process and increase the risk that NFIP full-risk premiums rates may not accurately reflect the underlying risk of flood loss. As a result, the premiums collected by FEMA for full-risk policies may not be sufficient to cover the risks associated with those policies. If the premiums are not sufficient, FEMA will likely have to continue to borrow from the Treasury and could face a future of financial instability because of its ongoing inability to cover claims and expenses.

FEMA's Process for Setting Subsidized Rates May Further Compromise the Ongoing Financial Stability of the Program

FEMA's rate-setting process for subsidized properties, which depends in part on the accuracy of the full-risk rates, has evolved over time. Currently, to determine subsidized rates, FEMA first subtracts the total amount that it expects to collect on full-risk rate premiums from the average historical loss year target—the minimum amount of premiums the program needs to collect to cover at least average annual losses based on historical loss data. The amount remaining from this calculation is the aggregate target amount of subsidized premiums that the program needs to collect. Then to set individual subsidized rates, FEMA officials consider their knowledge of flood risks, previous rate increases for various areas, and statutory limits on rate increases. Currently, the annual amount that NFIP collects in both full-risk and subsidized premiums is not enough to cover its operating costs, claim losses, and principal and interest payments to the Department of the Treasury. Without changes to its current rate-setting processes, NFIP premiums will be unlikely to be able to cover the program's claims, expenses, and debt, exposing the federal government and ultimately taxpayers to ever-greater financial risks, especially in years of catastrophic flooding.

The Process Used to Set Subsidized Rates Has Evolved over Time

In designing NFIP, Congress required that premiums for certain properties be offered at prices below those for full-risk premiums to encourage participation in the program and to ensure that premiums were affordable for existing structures in the floodplain. However, the statute does not provide a formula or methodology for setting the subsidies, leaving it up to the program to develop one. When the program began, NFIP administrators set the subsidized rates on the basis of what they believed would be affordable, but this process resulted in losses that had to be covered by borrowings as discussed previously. Some of the resulting deficit was later forgiven by Congress.

In 1981, NFIP administrators, after discussions with Congress, started setting NFIP's subsidized premium rates based on the average historical loss year calculations.[51] According to FEMA, this change allowed the agency to resist external pressures in setting premium rates and provided a more objective standard for determining subsidized rates. FEMA documents from most years between 2001 and 2006 state that the average historical loss year target, which is based on losses from previous years averaged over time, generally is considered a floor for premium collection. To account for the potential of catastrophic losses, and the additional funds required to pay such losses, FEMA sets premium rates so that the total premiums collected will be approximately 15 to 25 percent greater than the average historical loss year estimate.

However, FEMA can adjust, and has recently adjusted, the way it calculates the average historical loss year. Although loss years can vary markedly, none of those taken into account before 2005 included the kinds of catastrophic losses seen after Katrina, Rita, and Wilma. According to FEMA officials, including the 2005 losses in calculations of the average historical loss year would have resulted in premium increases well above the 10 percent statutory limit.[52] As a result, FEMA officials instituted a weighting factor for the 2005 losses, and as a result the full amount of the losses was not incorporated into the rate-setting model. According to FEMA officials, they incorporated losses of $2.1 billion of the estimated $23.2 billion in losses from 2005.[53] NFIP set the 2007 and 2008 flood insurance rates based on this modified methodology.

Although FEMA has incorporated more objective criteria against which to set rates for subsidized premiums, the process also depends on the accuracy of calculations for full-risk premiums.[54] After FEMA derives the full-risk premiums, it deducts the total amount of full-risk premiums that it expects to collect from the average historical loss year target; the remainder is the amount in premiums that it needs to collect from subsidized policies. Subsidized rates are then set based on this amount. Thus, the level of subsidized rates charged to policyholders depends, in part, on the full-risk premiums determined by FEMA. For example, if full-risk premiums are too low because they do not accurately reflect flood risk, the total amount FEMA will need to collect from subsidized policies will be higher, resulting in higher subsidized premiums.

Finally, according to FEMA, the rate-setting process for subsidized premiums also involves other considerations. Officials said once they had calculated the aggregate amount of subsidized premiums they would need, they determined the subsidized rate increases and ultimately the rates for the individual zones based on their knowledge and understanding of flood risks. FEMA officials told us that their decisions on how much to raise rates on various zones took into account concerns about the effect of increases on policyholders, the level and extent of past rate increases, and knowledge of relative flood risks in those areas. FEMA did not provide us with any written documentation describing how these decisions were reached. As mentioned previously, by law FEMA can raise rates on each zone by no more than 10 percent a year. Our review of FEMA documents show that FEMA raised rates significantly for a small number of policies and by very little for a large number of policies from 2002 through 2006. For example, FEMA raised rates by an average of more than 9 percent on about 1 percent of all NFIP policies—specifically, on certain subsidized policies located in high-risk coastal zones. In contrast, FEMA raised rates by an average of around 2 percent on 40 percent of total policies in high-risk zones that were paying full-risk rates.

Ultimately, the generally small increases will not help ensure NFIP's financial stability and may in fact decrease it by adding to its operating deficit.

NFIP's Current Rate-Setting Processes Result in Premiums That Are Not Sufficient to Cover Current Debt and Future Claims

The processes and policies that FEMA uses to set both full-risk and subsidized premium rates have contributed to NFIP's inability to generate enough in premiums to cover the program's operating costs, claims losses, and debt to the Treasury. From 1978 through 2004, NFIP had a net loss of $2 billion. These years had historically low flooding, but NFIP had yearly deficits for about half of these years. Over that period, Congress retired about $1.2 billion of this total debt. However, the introduction of average historical loss year targets in the 1980s resulted in a series of rate increases that contributed to a sizeable reduction of the net loss.

The 2005 hurricanes significantly altered NFIP's financial landscape. The 2005 hurricanes, especially Katrina, left the program with debt of more than $17.4 billion as of June 2008. To service the debt to the Treasury, FEMA owes two annual interest payments of around $365 million that are generally due in April and October of each year. FEMA officials told us that they were able to make the two payments in 2007 without borrowing because, according to FEMA documents, NFIP faced unusually light flooding in 2006 and 2007. In addition, FEMA made an unscheduled principal payment of $225 million in November 2007. However, in April 2008, FEMA borrowed $50 million to pay the $364 million interest payment owed to the Treasury. FEMA estimates that it will owe a total of $734 million in interest charges in fiscal year 2008.

FEMA officials informed us that they did not know whether NFIP would be able to make future interest payments without borrowing because of uncertainty about future flooding. According to FEMA documents, FEMA has paid $1.6 billion in interest to the Treasury since 2005. NFIP currently has about 5.6 million policies in force, resulting in approximately $2.6 billion in total premium. Historically, program expenses (excluding loss and allocated loss adjustment expenses) have averaged around 38 percent of premiums, or $1 billion of current total premium collection. As of June 2008, NFIP's average noncatastrophic historical loss year (which excludes Hurricanes Katrina, Rita, and Wilma) is about $1.3 billion. The combined outlays for loss and loss adjustment expenses of around $1.3 billion, administrative expenses of approximately $1 billion, and interest payments of approximately $0.7

billion exceed the program's current premium collection of approximately $2.6 billion. Under current conditions, it is unlikely that NFIP will be able to meet its interest payments in most years, and the program's debt will likely grow as the program borrows to meet the interest payments.

CONCLUSIONS

Over the years, FEMA has taken a number of steps to improve the rate-setting process, which was established more than two decades ago, but a number of factors raise questions about whether the resulting rates reflect the actual flood risk. First, potentially outdated and inaccurate data about flood probabilities, damage claims, and flood maps are increasing the risk that full-risk premiums do not reflect actual risk of flooding. Second, unlike many insurers in the private sector, FEMA has done little to understand the long-term impact of planned and ongoing development on damage estimates. While this is due, in part, to the fact that FEMA lacks the authority to factor potential or long-term development into potential flood damage, FEMA has not, for example, evaluated how such developments could affect the accuracy of its maps. Finally, FEMA's continued use of a nationwide rating structure that combines zones across geographic areas despite the substantial growth of the program introduces additional uncertainties. While additional analysis of the data is needed, our analysis found that some patterns in historical claims and premiums collected raise questions about whether this approach is still appropriate and reasonable given the growth in the program. Collectively, these factors call into question the accuracy of the full-risk rates generated by FEMA's rate model. By updating elements of its flood rate model and certain rate-setting policies, FEMA could help ensure that data used in its model such as flood probabilities, damage estimates, and information from flood maps are as accurate as possible. In addition, by reconsidering risk aggregation across flood zones and the effects of development and climate change into the rate-setting process, FEMA has the opportunity to make its model more robust and increase the accuracy of its rates.

Similarly, FEMA's policy of allowing properties that have been remapped to higher-risk zones to retain lower rates results in rates that do not accurately reflect flood risk. Because the premiums are not based on the actual risk of flooding, these policyholders are receiving a subsidy from other policyholders in the same zone and the federal government—and ultimately from taxpayers.

We are encouraged that FEMA plans to implement a monitoring process for grandfathered properties, which would allow it to better determine the impact of these properties on the program's financial stability. However, because FEMA plans to track only grandfathered properties in the future, not existing properties, it will not be able to fully evaluate whether grandfathering actually is fulfilling the desired goals in a cost-effective way. Unless there is a full accounting of grandfathered properties, these properties expose the program to an unknown level of risk. Prompt attention to this issue could allow NFIP to refine its rate-setting process in the short term and provide valuable information on the effects of its policy decision on the financial stability of the program.

Finally, FEMA's rate-setting process for subsidized properties depends in part on the accuracy of full-risk rates, raising concerns about how these rates are calculated as well. While FEMA is statutorily required to subsidize rates, the method used for setting subsidized rates has evolved from one that is based largely on affordability to one based on the average historical loss year estimate. The resulting subsidized premiums continue to be a financial strain on NFIP and contribute to its ongoing financial instability. Based on NFIP's current premium collections, it is not only unlikely that NFIP will be unable to repay its debt but also unlikely that it will be able to make interest payments in years with any significant amount of flood activities, and the program's debt will likely grow as it borrows to meet the interest payments, as was the case in mid-2008. Unless NFIP addresses issues with its rate-setting processes, premiums collected will remain insufficient in the face of future flood losses—even in average flood loss years—leaving both the program and taxpayers at increased financial risk. While a robust rate-setting process that accurately reflects underlying flood risk is a key step in helping to improve the long-term financial stability of NFIP, no process can ensure that premiums will always cover losses because of the potential for large claim losses associated with catastrophic events. However, any efforts to improve the accuracy of the premiums charged by the program will help reduce the financial risk to which the federal government and, ultimately, taxpayers are exposed from the flood insurance program.

RECOMMENDATIONS FOR EXECUTIVE ACTION

We recommend that the Secretary of the Department of Homeland Security direct FEMA to take steps to ensure that its rate-setting methods and the data it uses to set rates result in full-risk premiums rates that accurately reflect the risk of losses from flooding. These steps should include, for example, verifying the accuracy of flood probabilities, damage estimates, and flood maps; ensuring that the effects of long-term planned and ongoing development, as well as climate change, are reflected in the flood probabilities used; and reevaluating the practice of aggregating risks across zones.

We also recommend that the Secretary of the Department of Homeland Security direct FEMA to ensure that information is collected on the location, number, and losses associated with existing and newly created grandfathered properties in NFIP and to analyze the financial impact of these properties on the flood insurance program.

AGENCY COMMENTS AND OUR EVALUATION

We provided the Secretary of Homeland Security with a draft of this chapter for review and comment. On October 14, 2008, FEMA provided written comments on a draft of this chapter. FEMA generally concurred with both of the report's recommendations but had two reservations about our recommendation to ensure that FEMA's rate-setting methods result in full-risk rates that accurately reflect the risk of losses from flooding. Moreover, while FEMA noted that the report makes a number of constructive suggestions, it took exception to some of our analyses and characterizations, which it believes overstate their potential impact on the accuracy of the rate-setting process. These comments are summarized below and FEMA's letter is reprinted in appendix III. FEMA also provided us with technical comments, which we incorporated as appropriate.

FEMA generally concurred with our recommendation that it take steps to ensure that FEMA's rate-setting methods result in full-risk rates that accurately reflect the risk of losses from flooding, but expressed two reservations. First, it said that the report taken as a whole presents a view of the accuracy of the current FEMA rate-setting process that is "far too negative," especially given the complexity and difficulty of setting flood insurance premium rates. We recognize that determining full-risk premium rates for flood insurance is an inherently challenging process, especially given the potential for catastrophic losses in any given year. However, in objectively reviewing the rate-setting process and applying generally accepted principles of insurance and actuarial rate setting, we found a number of areas that, when considered collectively, raise questions about the accuracy of the resulting rates and highlight areas that warrant additional analysis by FEMA. For example, for the period of 1978-2003, prior to the catastrophic losses resulting from the hurricanes of 2005, the low to moderate full-risk zones had a cumulative deficit of approximately $685 million. This deficit would seem to indicate that the rates for these risk classes were not adequate to cover the expected losses—a basic actuarial principle. And while the entire full-risk portion of the program did have an overall surplus of approximately $382 million over the same period, this would appear only to indicate the existence of a large cross subsidy between the rated zones, which reinforces our recommendation that FEMA revisit its nationwide class-rating system.

Second, FEMA said that the report does not accurately present the status of its map modernization efforts and their impact on premium rates. Specifically, with respect to map modernization, FEMA stated that (1) our characterization of the progress on the updating of flood maps was misleading; (2) we overstate the impact of older maps on rate setting; and (3) we failed to note that FEMA allows communities to reflect future conditions in flood maps the communities help develop. With respect to the progress of map modernization, FEMA provided the data that we presented in the report, which represents a status of modernization efforts to date. FEMA appears to take issue with measuring the status of map modernization in terms of the number of flood maps that had been updated. We note that in its comment letter, FEMA analyzed progress in terms of the population living within areas covered by updated maps. Each form of analysis provides a different picture of the progress of map modernization, and we have now added FEMA's data to reflect population measures in order to present an additional perspective. With respect to the impact of older maps on rate setting, FEMA states that older maps are not always outdated, and that in many areas the flood hazard has not changed or is possibly decreasing. While some maps may not have changed over the past 10 to 15 years, it is uncertain how many maps fall into this category and FEMA provided no analysis to support this contention. In addition, as we note in our report, FEMA stated that it undertook map modernization for several reasons, including that flood hazard conditions are dynamic and many flood maps may not reflect recent development or environmental changes; updated maps can take advantage of revised data and improved technologies for identifying flood hazards; and up-to-date maps support a flood insurance program that is more aligned with actual risks. These reasons would seem to reflect a concern that older maps can become outdated. Moreover, we also note that FEMA plans to update its maps every 5 years to make sure they remain accurate. With respect to allowing communities to voluntarily reflect future conditions in flood maps, we were not made aware of these efforts in time to evaluate them for inclusion in this chapter but we plan to review these efforts in future work. FEMA had additional comments on how we characterized its rate-setting process. We address these comments below.

First, FEMA stated that our finding that probability curves for floodwaters exceeding a specific elevation had not been updated since the 1980s was unfounded because these probabilities are relative to the base flood elevation (BFE), and BFEs are revised as flood maps are updated. As we noted in our report, flood risk experts told us that flood probabilities are likely to change as land use, infrastructure, and weather patterns change. As a result, even if the probability curves are adjusted to reflect a new BFE, other changes since the 1980s could result in the probability curves themselves no longer being accurate. FEMA stated that it prepared a sensitivity analysis that showed that reestimating the probability curves would have a minimal impact on rates. We were not provided this analysis until FEMA gave us its comments on this chapter, and therefore cannot comment on the accuracy of the analysis. Nonetheless, it illustrates the type of analysis that FEMA should perform periodically to ensure the integrity of its rate-setting process and are encouraged by this effort. Finally, while we understand that the data used to develop probability curves were based on detailed engineering studies, available flood data, simulations, and professional judgments, neither FEMA nor the Corps was able to provide us with the specific data set used to develop the original probability curves. As a result, we could not review the reliability of those data.

Second, in response to FEMA comments about the Corps' use of the hydrologic model that underlies FEMA's flood insurance rate-setting process, we have clarified the language in our report to make clear that while the Corps has revised its model for estimating flood damage, it continues to use the hydrologic model.

Third, FEMA stated that we dismissed its contention that it is adequately pricing the premiums for the class of business that includes grandfathered properties. Considering the class of grandfathered properties as a subset of policyholders, owners of grandfathered properties pay less than full-risk premiums. Although FEMA may raise premiums for others to compensate for the potential shortfall from this subset, the extent and effect of this cross-subsidization deserves scrutiny and should be analyzed. FEMA concurred with our recommendation to gather additional information on grandfathered properties and analyze their financial impact on NFIP.

Fourth, FEMA challenged our discussion about the number of risk groups used for rate setting and contended that we failed to consider the complexity and cost of using more refined risk classifications. We did recognize and consider the challenges associated with using more refined risk groups and therefore did not specifically recommend that FEMA change its risk rating system. Instead, we recommended that FEMA reevaluate its practice of aggregating risks across zones in light of the program's expansion to determine whether the current risk groups are still relevant. As we noted in our report, FEMA has not revisited its class rating approach since its inception, when it had around 2 million policyholders. The program currently has over 5.5 million policyholders. Since then, there have been significant changes in both the number and location of properties insured by NFIP that would warrant revisiting of FEMA's approach to aggregating risks.

Finally, concerning our analysis of historical claims data, FEMA commented that we did not compare historical losses across states to a theoretical distribution and stated that it believed that the distribution we observed could be explained by analyzing the interaction of the variability of flood risk and the declining number of policyholders receiving discounted premiums. However, FEMA provided no analytical basis for this belief and has not conducted any such analysis to support this assertion. Moreover, FEMA also commented that until such analysis is done, it cannot be sure of the results. We would encourage FEMA to build upon our analysis and continue to explore ways to leverage existing data to evaluate the effective of its rate-setting process and identify ways to strengthen the process. In addition, FEMA expressed its disappointment that we did not include the results of our analysis of losses across states in our report. While we included a shorter version of this analysis in the body of the report, we continued to present the full results of our analysis in appendix II of the report.

As agreed with your office, unless you publicly announce the contents of this chapter earlier, we plan no further distribution of this chapter until 30 days from the report date. At that time, we will provide copies to the Chairman, Senate Committee on Banking, Housing and Urban Affairs; the Chairman and Ranking Member of the Senate Committee on Homeland Security and Governmental Affairs; the Chairman and Ranking Member of the House

Committee on Financial Services; the Chairman and Ranking Member of the House Committee on Homeland Security; and other interested committees. We are also sending a copy of this chapter to the Secretary of Homeland Security and other interested parties. In addition, the report will available at no charge on our Web site at http://www.gao.gov.

Sincerely,

Orice Williams
Director, Financial Markets and Community Investment

APPENDIX I. SCOPE AND METHODOLOGY

To assess the Federal Emergency Management Agency's (FEMA) rate-setting process and determine whether it produces rates that accurately reflect the risk of flooding for properties that do not receive subsidies, we reviewed and analyzed FEMA's model for evaluating potential flood damage to properties as well as the methods used for assessing risk and setting premium rates for policyholders. We discussed FEMA's method for rate setting with officials from FEMA, the National Oceanic and Atmospheric Administration, U.S. Army Corps of Engineers (the Corps), and the U.S Geological Survey. We met with risk-modeling agencies, academics and the American Academy of Actuaries to obtain views on FEMA's model and information on private sector flood-risk-modeling methods and data sources. We met with FEMA officials to obtain relevant information and data on FEMA's Map Modernization program. We reviewed FEMA documents and met with FEMA officials in order to understand FEMA's process and policies for grandfathering properties and the impact on the program. We analyzed FEMA's premiums and claims data to determine the number of high-loss years on a state-by-state basis in order to assess each state's financial impact on NFIP. In order to conduct the state loss analysis, we reviewed the claims and premium data from NFIP's BureauNet database. For premium data, we used "Historical Policy Summary" and "All States" each year, individually from 1978 through 2007. For the claims data, we used "Claims Data Summary" and obtained Closed Claims, CWOP, and Open Claims by using the "State Name" and "Calendar Year" sort fields. These numbers were then adjusted for inflation using historic calendar year gross domestic product (GDP) data. Finally, we subtracted claims values from the premiums values, and sorted the states by the number of years in which each state experienced a high-loss year, or a year in which claims exceeded premiums. We also calculated aggregate inflation adjusted claims amounts for each state. Because of the catastrophic effects of the 2005 hurricanes, we also calculated pre-Katrina (1978 through 2004) numbers, which were displayed in table 3. To assess the impact of the rate-setting process and other factors on NFIP's long-term financial stability, we interviewed officials to obtain specific information on NFIP's current and past financial status. We also collected and analyzed information on NFIP's financial status and reviewed existing FEMA documents.

To evaluate the process that NFIP uses to set subsidized rates, we interviewed officials from FEMA to obtain the methodology used to assess total premium needs and set subsidized rates. We collected and analyzed information on FEMA's process for setting rates for subsidized flood insurance and reviewed documents on NFIP program subsidies and recommendations to eliminate them. We also reviewed academic and other studies of studies of flood risk and flood insurance including reviews from the Congressional Research Service and the Congressional Budget Office.

We conducted this work from December 2007 to September 2008 in accordance with generally accepted government auditing standards. Those standards require that we plan and perform the audit to obtain sufficient, appropriate evidence to provide a reasonable basis for our findings and conclusions based on our audit objectives. We note that the evidence obtained provides a reasonable basis for our findings and conclusions based on our audit objectives.

APPENDIX II. STATE-BY-STATE ANALYSIS OF CLAIMS AND PREMIUMS DATA

Because rare but large events can account for a large portion of the long-term aggregate experience, we supplemented the aggregate data analysis with the annual high-loss year analysis. Nevertheless, on a cumulative basis for 1978-2004, a period before Hurricanes Katrina and Rita policyholders in several states received markedly more in claims paid out than NFIP collected from them in premiums.[55] Five of the nine states with at least 8 high-loss years—Alabama, Missouri, Mississippi, Texas, and West Virginia—had more in aggregate claims than policyholders paid out in aggregate premiums. Five other states—Kentucky, Minnesota, North Carolina, North Dakota, and Oklahoma—had aggregate claims exceeding aggregate premiums, all of them experiencing between 5 and 7 high-loss years. By expanding the totals to include all years through 2007, Louisiana joins the other nine states with aggregate claims exceeding aggregate premiums, primarily because of Hurricanes Katrina and Rita. On the other extreme, three states—California, Florida, and New Jersey—had aggregate premiums exceed aggregate claims by more than $1 billion, with Florida having an $8 billion surplus.

Table 4. Claims and Premiums Data (in constant 2007 dollars), 1978–2007

State	1978-2004 Premiums minus claims	1978-2007 premiums minus claims	1978-2007 Number of years that claims exceeded premiums
Missouri	($384,344,855)	(350,344,220)	11
West Virginia	(146,896,812)	(118,874,830)	11
Mississippi	(40,584,822)	(2,498,544,520)	10
Louisiana*	428,383,041	(11,777,260,456)	10
Texas*	(728,796,632)	(222,265,084)	9
Alabama	(505,212,107)	(746,166,995)	9
Illinois	90,321,291	162,050,972	9
Ohio	101,547,985	100,111,514	9
New Hampshire	36,648,547	21,531,170	8
Oklahoma	(18,199,240)	(25,642,039)	7
South Dakota	5,295,971	8,404,092	7
Kansas	20,948,695	20,247,134	7
Washington	85,320,803	66,244,958	7
Indiana	131,316,681	166,958,946	7
North Carolina	(169,814,330)	(8,457,439)	6
Minnesota	(63,190,911)	(52,511,837)	6
Arkansas	52,001,936	74,966,251	6
Pennsylvania	84,458,562	23,509,354	6
Connecticut	209,580,515	266,043,856	6
North Dakota	(111,305,692)	(103,851,773)	5
Kentucky	(56,850,302)	(42,009,555)	5
District of Columbia	1,030,982	1,734,592	5
Maine	39,784,737	46,807,732	5
Tennessee	47,004,528	82,337,301	5
Virginia	60,909,715	172,548,603	5
Rhode Island	127,856,579	152,323,748	5
New York	574,475,012	648,183,499	5
Iowa	15,016,861	32,394,824	4

Table 4 (Continued)

Massachusetts	165,750,753	227,224,840	4
New Jersey*	1,071,199,191	1,271,686,111	4
California*	2,042,968,575	2,431,519,768	4
Montana	20,618,089	26,387,334	3
Maryland	63,198,089	139,162,073	3
Wisconsin	68,781,850	90,093,940	3
Nebraska	77,523,305	98,540,480	3
Delaware	79,318,937	115,022,170	3
Michigan	173,141,113	222,803,680	3
Hawaii	185,512,050	245,450,036	3
Arizona	204,216,092	251,713,046	3
Georgia	265,586,974	389,183,828	3
Utah	15,372,336	21,207,776	2
Wyoming	16,597,320	21,134,460	2
Nevada	70,283,808	82,293,838	2
Vermont	23,425,436	30,590,342	1
Idaho	32,991,914	42,892,136	1
Oregon	104,014,018	133,186,375	1
South Carolina	313,400,772	590,371,633	1
Florida*	8,035,673,802	9,938,638,592	1
Alaska	23,003,446	27,770,628	0
New Mexico	79,909,374	97,876,034	0
Colorado	$135,763,975	$170,139,136	0

Source: GAO analysis of FEMA data.

Note: We analyzed two time periods so we could separately consider the impact of the 2005 Hurricanes Katrina, Rita, and Wilma. *Denotes the five states with the highest number of subsidized policies.

As noted in the report, additional study would be required to determine whether policyholders in some states with lower losses are paying a higher premium than is appropriate for their risk, and others paying too little. For example, our analysis did not control for differences in the type of policy purchased, such as the mix of certain property types across states and insurance coverage amounts, which could affect both premiums and claims. In addition, we did not control for differences in the mix of subsidized and full-risk policies or the impact of subsidized premiums on our results, which could also affect the results. For example, some states have a relatively large number or proportion of subsidized properties (including grandfathered properties) that generally would lead to higher expected claims relative to premiums, but we were unable to link the separate NFIP claims and premiums data at the state and zone levels in a way that would allow us to perform a more refined analysis. The limitations in setting full-risk rates that we have discussed could result in systematic mispricing relative to risk that becomes apparent only over long periods; however, our analysis included both subsidized and full-risk properties, and so the results should be considered in this context.

APPENDIX III. COMMENTS FROM FEMA

Homeland Security

October 14, 2008

Ms. Orice M. Williams
Director
Financial Markets and Community Investment
U.S. Government Accountability Office
441 G St., NW
Washington, DC 20548

Dear Ms. Williams:

The U.S. Department of Homeland Security (DHS) appreciates the opportunity to review and comment on the U.S. Government Accountability Office's (GAO) draft report GAO-09-12 titled *FLOOD INSURANCE: FEMA's Rate-Setting Process Warrants Attention* (250387).

While the GAO raises valid concerns, DHS believes that the analysis does not grasp some generally accepted principles of insurance and actuarial rate-setting and misrepresents the status of the Map Modernization effort and its impact on rate adequacy. We appreciate GAO presenting a generally accurate description of the methodology and National Flood Insurance Program (NFIP) premium rates. Few individuals understand the model and methodology and we appreciate GAO staff learning many of the intricacies of the rate-setting process. The report has made a number of constructive suggestions, some of which DHS is actively pursuing, others that we will take under advisement and, as discussed below, a few with which we disagree.

GAO raised concerns in several areas of the NFIP rate-setting methodology, including: (1) data quality of probability estimates, claim severity estimates, and maps; (2) future conditions impacted by climate change, erosion, and future development; and (3) underwriting results. DHS believes that GAO is overestimating the potential impact of each of these areas. Below, is our response to the major points highlighted in the report; they are sorted by the headings used in the report.

Data Used to Determine Flood Probabilities Have Not Been Updated Since the 1970s and 1980s

GAO expressed concern that the probability curves for floodwater exceeding a specific elevation had not been updated since the 1980s. Since these probabilities are expressed relative to the Base Flood Elevation (BFE), GAO concerns are unfounded. As flood maps are updated to reflect revised BFEs, the PELV curves are automatically re-benchmarked to the revised BFEs. Since the various PELV curves for zones A01 through A30 are based on the relative elevation difference between a "10-year flood" and a "100-year flood" it is very likely that the floodwater depths for the "250-year flood" or the "500-year flood" remain stable within a specific zone. If the water depth for the "500-year flood" changes significantly in relation to the BFE, then it is likely that the "10-year flood" has also changed in relation to the BFE, resulting in a flood zone change. When the zone changes, the PELV associated with the new zone would be reflected in the appropriate probabilities. FEMA updates its probabilities by re-estimating the annual chance of exceeding the one percent flood (i.e., the BFE). FEMA prepared a sensitivity analysis of the impact on rates and preliminarily concluded there would be a minimal impact.

<u>The Claims Data Used in the Model May Be Inaccurate</u>
Water Depth Data

FEMA agrees with the suggestion to improve the collection of data on water depth in the structure. GAO correctly describes FEMA's method of handling claims where the depth of water is missing or erroneously reported as zero in the claims database. As GAO notes, the effect will be to overstate the flood damage for flood events with only a few inches of water in the structure. However, GAO points out that the impact is unknown for the flood events of greater water depth. FEMA believes this is worth investigating and will conduct a sensitivity analysis of the impact of this type of claim on the rate setting method. As the GAO report points out, FEMA has reviewed the impact of such errors in the past and believes that they generally would result in more conservative premium rates.

Army Corps of Engineers Use of NFIP Claims Data

GAO contends that the United States Army Corps of Engineers (USACE) has moved away from the hydrologic model that underlies the NFIP rate model and developed independent damage estimates for their use.

We reviewed the USACE document ER-1105-2-101. We disagree with the characterization that it no longer relies on the hydrologic model described in FEMA material. The document describes the change they made to their methodology. The "Standard Project Flood" (SPF) is defined in several documents. In the context of ER 1105-2-100 and risk analysis guidance, the SPF is no longer a valid design target. Instead, a full range of floods, including those that would exceed the SPF is to be used in formulation and evaluation of alternatives. Based on that description, we believe that their revision now much more closely follows FEMA methodology. The USACE's historical methodology seems to model only one possible loss event, which they labeled the SPF. By contrast, the NFIP Rate Model has always considered "a full range of floods" by use of the PELV and PELV500 curves. Instead, based on our read of that document, it appears that the U.S. Army Corps of Engineers has revised its model to resemble closely the NFIP Rate Model. We believe that new approach, which considers a full range of floods, is a much more robust approach which is the reason why we have always used it.

GAO states that "As a result [of NFIP claims data quality issues], the Corps began to collect its own damage data, which FEMA now uses to supplement its own data." It is true that FEMA has always used the USACE's data to supplement NFIP claims data where NFIP claims data is too thin to be actuarially credible. However, we provide in Table 1 an analysis of the previous and newly revised USACE data compared to NFIP claims data. It appears either that the USACE is still using NFIP data or that the alternative data that they now use is very similar to NFIP data.

Table 1 - Comparison of USACE Studies to NFIP Data
One story, no basement structures
Percent damage by depth

Depth	1973 USACE Study	Revised USACE Study	NFIP Experience
-1	-	2.50	11.23
0	7.00	13.40	19.52
1	10.00	23.30	22.34
2	14.00	32.10	31.16
3	26.00	40.10	37.55
4	28.00	47.10	48.26
5	29.00	53.20	60.11
6	41.00	58.60	58.43
7	43.00	63.20	70.50
8	44.00	67.20	68.73
9	45.00	70.50	72.23
10	46.00	73.20	79.68

<u>Maps that Provide Information for Base Flood Elevations Remain Substantially Out-of-Date Despite Modernization Efforts</u>

Maps will never be fully up-to-date everywhere in the country and thus never fully reflect the current flood risk. FEMA believes that GAO significantly understates the overall quality of current maps and, as a result, is over-estimating the possible impact of these older maps on pricing. FEMA believes that the Hydrologic Rate Model used in estimating rates has sufficient additional conservatism to compensate for these factors and can state with confidence that the premiums from the Rate Model are a reasonable estimate of the full risk premium based on the full range of flood loss probabilities.

FEMA is concerned that the figures GAO references regarding the number of maps that are at least 5, 10, or 15 years old may be misleading. Many of those maps are still being updated as part of Map Modernization. It generally takes between two to three years to finalize flood map changes in coordination with state and local governments. That being the case, current map age can be misleading. As of March 2008, approximately 68% of the nation's population has already received updated maps that met, exceed, or at least approach the map quality targets of Map Modernization, while another 27% of the population has received a preliminary map. By the end of FY 2010, FEMA anticipates that at least 92% of the nation's population will have a modernized flood map.

GAO seems to have a concern that an old map is an incorrect map that understates the flood risk and therefore adversely affects insurance pricing. Older maps are not always outdated. In many areas with older flood maps, the flood hazard has not significantly changed or is possibly decreasing. Further, there are instances where areas have not been re-studied because the stream gauge or historical data does not include any new flooding events, even of small magnitude, so there is no additional data with which to update the maps.

GAO has also expressed concern about the possible deterioration of a map's quality between the scheduled five-year update. While this happens in some areas of the country for a variety of reasons, it is also true that some States or local communities attempt to lessen the impact of the changes in the flood risk. When deterioration of the flood risk occurs, local communities are required to communicate to FEMA as soon as practical, but no later than six months, appropriate data to use to update the community's maps to reflect current flooding conditions. In this way, FEMA assures that maps are updated more frequently than every five years to reflect changing conditions. These and other changes to the maps are usually done through the Letter of Map Amendment/Letter of Map Revision process. These amendments and revisions currently average about 22,000 a year.

GAO fails to note the advancements FEMA has made in allowing communities to reflect future conditions in maps they develop. Currently, communities can choose to use future conditions hydrology for mapping per a Federal Register notice published on November 27, 2001. Future conditions hydrology are based on projected land-use conditions of the watershed, which could increase surface water runoff such as an increase in impervious areas created by future parking lots or structures or future construction/improvement of drainage networks that accompany urbanization. While FEMA does not require future conditions mapping, we are working to encourage local communities to adopt it voluntarily through these procedures and through NFIP Community Rating System credits.

FEMA Does Not Track the Number or Location of Remapped Grandfathered Properties That Pay Less Than Full Risk Premiums

The report correctly describes the current FEMA program of grandfathering currently. GAO acknowledges FEMA's belief that it is adequately pricing the premiums for the class of business which includes the grandfathered policies because the methodology that the NFIP uses in setting rates for the X-Standard risk group includes these grandfathered properties. However, GAO dismisses this contention. We allow X-Standard policies to continue to use the X-Zone for rating purpose but set the overall premium level that we estimate to reflect the full-risk of that risk group as a whole. The report does not mention that the grandfathered X-Standard premium is substantially higher than the previous X-Preferred Risk that most of these policyholders had been charged. FEMA provided GAO premium charts that showed that the X-Zone standard premium is now higher than the premium for some AE-Zone compliant structures. In addition a significant portion of these grandfathered policies are older Pre-FIRM policies that would be eligible for subsidized premiums and would no longer be part of a risk class that is charged on average their full-risk premiums.

FEMA Does Not Consider Risk Factors Such as Erosion and Climate Change When Setting Flood Insurance Rates

Although FEMA has not investigated the issue of climate change and its impact on the NFIP in totality, we conducted a study in 1991 that focused on one aspect of climate change, sea level rise. The study, titled *Projected Impact of Relative Sea Level Rise on the National*

Flood Insurance Program[1], concluded that the NFIP would not be impacted significantly under sea level rise scenarios put forth in the first Intergovernmental Panel on Climate Change (IPCC) report released in 1990. FEMA has initiated a new study on climate change titled, *Impact of Climate Change on the NFIP and Improving Coastal Floodplain Mapping*. The study will include an investigation of the impacts of sea level rise, changes in hurricane frequency and intensity, and changes in precipitation patterns and how they might affect the NFIP. FEMA will use the latest information contained in the most recent IPCC and Climate Change Science Program (CCSP) projections and findings in the conduct of this study. We expect to complete the study in early 2010 and will carefully evaluate its findings to determine how to best account for climate change in setting flood insurance rates.

In the absence of the authority to establish erosion zones, FEMA has taken actions based on the Heinz Center[2] study on coastal erosion, which projected increased damages due to the effects of long-term coastal erosion over a 60-year period. We have increased rates for all V-Zone properties at a pace commensurate with the Heinz Center projections, since we cannot explicitly identify those properties most at risk from erosion.

The FEMA Rating System Combines and Averages Many Different Risks to Create Nationwide Rates

GAO concerns regarding the current amount of risk groups are misplaced. GAO correctly notes that the flood risk for individual policyholders varies within the current risk groups. This is also true for risk groups in the private insurance industry. In establishing risk groups, FEMA must balance the administrative complexity of a highly refined number of risk groups against the degree of heterogeneity of risk within those groups. FEMA continues to believe that we have found the appropriate balance. GAO does not consider the amount of complexity that their recommendation for more highly refined risk groups would create. The size of the rate manual would increase many-fold, as would the difficulty of making accurate zone determinations in those communities that have a variety of A-numbered zones.

FEMA has considered the implications on our current risk group classifications if future legislative changes require the NFIP to reduce significantly the classes of buildings that are eligible for premium subsidies. Whereas, the current risk groups may not result in significant cross-subsidization among compliant structures that will probably not be true for older non-compliant structures. Simply extending the current practice of manually rating non-compliant structures to these older structures, will not work since FEMA does not have the staff to support the increased workload. FEMA has begun considering how to revise its rate structure if future subsidy reduction is mandated.

Our Analysis of Historical Claims and Premium Data Raises Questions about a Potential Mismatch between Rates and Risk

GAO conclusions from this analysis appear to inject its expectations as to how the results should have behaved if rates were actuarial. We believe the NFIP actual experience compares to estimates of the theoretical distribution, which GAO did not do. Unfortunately, FEMA did

[1] FEMA, *Projected Impact of Relative Sea Level Rise on the National Flood Insurance Program*, October 1991, available at http://www.epa.gov/climatechange/effects/downloads/flood_insurance.pdf.
[2] The Heinz Center, *Evaluation of Erosion Hazards*, April 2000, available at http://www.fema.gov/pdf/library/erosion.pdf.

not have time to develop a theoretical distribution to make this comparison. We believe that the distribution of the results that GAO observed in their analysis is explained by understanding the interaction of the variable flood risk and the greatly declining percentage through the years of policyholders who receive discounted premiums. However, until a more refined model is constructed, we will not know which is correct.

GAO had prepared an analysis of how often the annual loss experience for a state was above or below the median result for the year. We were disappointed to see GAO did not include this analysis in the report. FEMA believes that with more refinement and adjustments the analysis had the potential to be useful.

The FEMA Process for Setting Subsidized Rates May Further Compromise the Ongoing Financial Stability of the Program

The report is critical of FEMA methodology for setting the premium rates for the subsidized policies. The process used to set subsidized rates has evolved over time, and the report accurately describes the current process. We consider many factors in setting subsidized rates, and the 2005 hurricanes have had a major impact on those considerations. FEMA is in the process of reviewing its methodology with respect to the premium rates of the subsidized business. We are looking for guidance from the Congress on who should continue to be eligible for subsidized rates and the level of subsidy provided to them.

DHS generally concurs with both of the report's recommendation with two reservations. Following are our recommendation-specific comments; technical comments were provided under separate cover.

GAO Recommendation 1: We recommend that FEMA take steps to ensure that its rate setting methods and data used to set rates result in full-risk premiums rates that accurately reflect the risk of losses from flooding. For example, verifying the accuracy of flood probabilities, damage estimates, and flood maps; ensuring that the effects of long-term planned and ongoing development, as well as climate change, are reflected in the flood probabilities used; and reevaluating the practice of aggregating risks across zones.

DHS Response: Concur with reservation. In general, FEMA concurs with the first recommendation with two reservations. One, the GAO commentary taken as a whole presents far too negative a picture of the accuracy of the current NFIP pricing model and methodology. FEMA notes that the NFIP rate-setting process has evolved over a number of years and is dependent on many complicated inputs, estimations, modeling techniques and actuarial judgments. This type of process is always an inexact science, and we are always looking for, and will continue to incorporate, improvements in each of those areas as the needs and our resources allow. Two, FEMA believes that the report does not accurately present the status of the Map Modernization effort and its impact on rate adequacy.

There are many lines of insurance where precise measurement is practically impossible. As an example, in Workers' Compensation insurance there is uncertainty as to how workplace safety will vary over time due to technological advancements, workplace safety measures, the size of court awards to injured plaintiffs, future interest rates that will affect benefit levels, and future medical costs. The challenges and practical impossibility of precisely quantifying these factors do not mean that workers compensation insurance is not actuarially sound.

Rather in workers compensation insurance, like flood insurance, actuaries make judgments to establish rates that deal with a variety of uncertainties. Like Workers' Compensation insurance, where there is imprecision in estimating the parameters of the Rate Model or in the application of those indicated rates in the real world of selling flood insurance, FEMA actuaries have a history of consulting with other subject matter experts, such as hydrologic and/or hydraulic scientists, and the building science and mapping experts within FEMA. This has allowed them to estimate appropriately the impact of these parameters of the rate model.

GAO Recommendation 2: We also recommend that the Secretary of Homeland Security direct FEMA to ensure that information is collected on the location, number, and losses associated with existing and newly created grandfather properties in NFIP and to analyze the financial impact of these properties on the flood insurance.

DHS Response: Concur. DHS agrees with the need to start identifying the number of grandfather policies. While there are sound public policy reasons why the NFIP introduced and has maintained its grandfathered policies, there are also benefits to charging these policyholders a premium that is close to their specific risk instead of a premium based on a wider class of risks. Such as change would more fully communicate to the property owner the flood risk faced and encourage the property owner to take action to reduce that risk.

We are implementing a data collection effort for all newly grandfathered policies effective on or after May 1, 2009. However, collecting such data on currently insured structures is far more difficult. FEMA intends to work out a methodology to do that and to develop the financial analysis recommended.

FEMA believes that the NFIP rate setting process is sound and is conducted in accordance with the body of statutory and regulatory authority governing the NFIP and within the standards of actuarial practice and acknowledge there is always room for improvement. We thank the GAO staff for presenting in this report a number of constructive suggestions for improvements in our rate-setting process.

U.S. Department of Homeland Security would like to thank you for the opportunity to review and provide comments on the draft report. We look forward to working with you on future homeland security issues.

Sincerely,

Jerald E. Levine
Director
Departmental DHS GAO/OIG Liaison Office

End Notes

[1] GAO, *High-Risk Program: National Flood Insurance Program*, GAO-06-497T (Washington D.C.: Mar. 15, 2006).

[2] To assess the risk of flooding, FEMA uses Flood Insurance Rate Maps (FIRM) that show the level of flood risk in communities that participate in NFIP.

[3] BureauNet is the system that FEMA uses to collect, manage, and access its policy, claims, and policyholder data.

[4] We use the term "full risk" to describe rates that FEMA refers to as "actuarial." These are the risk premium rates specified in the National Flood Insurance Act of 1968, which FEMA

maintains accurately reflect flood risk and thus are not explicitly subsidized—that is, these rates contemplate the full range of loss potential including catastrophic levels, according to FEMA. The National Flood Insurance Act of 1968, as amended, is codified at 42 U.S.C. §§ 4001 *et. seq.*

[5] A hydrologic model is a static or dynamic representation of the process that affects surface water runoff. Hydrologic models are used to describe present conditions or predict future behavior of the hydrologic regime at a specific area of land that "caches" and "releases" surface water runoff (referred to as catchment.) Examples of hydrologic model inputs are precipitation and snow melt and example outputs are stream discharge and evapotranspiration. According to insurance market participants, to generate the loss estimates, private insurance companies and state authorities use models, which are computer programs with large databases that catalog the past incidence and severity of natural catastrophes, as well as proprietary insurance company data on policies written in particular states or areas. Using the estimates provided by these computer programs, insurers can attempt to manage their exposures in particular high-risk areas. See GAO, *Catastrophe Risk: U.S. and European Approaches to Insure Natural Catastrophe and Insurance Risks*, GAO-05-199 (Washington, D.C.: Feb. 28, 2005)

[6] A flood zone is an area that is designated to have a predicted likelihood of experiencing flood damage.

[7] SFHAs, which are depicted on NFIP maps, represent the land area that would be submerged by the floodwaters of the "base," or 1 percent annual chance of flood. The SFHA is also referred to as the 100-year or 1 percent floodplain. NFIP's floodplain management regulations must be enforced in, and the mandatory purchase of flood insurance applies to, SFHAs.

[8] A substantial improvement is any reconstruction, rehabilitation, addition, or other improvement of a structure, the cost of which equals or exceeds 50 percent of the market value of the structure before the "start of construction" of the improvement. If a building is "substantially damaged" or "substantially improved," it must be brought into compliance with local flood damage prevention regulations, including elevating the building to or above the 100-year flood elevation.

[9] The BFE is the elevation relative to mean sea level at which there is a 1 percent chance of floodwaters rising in a given year. The level of the BFE within a community can change throughout the floodplain.

[10] Some programs are also designated as having Emergency Program status. The Emergency Flood Insurance Program is intended as a program to provide a first layer amount of insurance on all insurable structures before the effective date of the initial FIRM.

[11] The rate-setting methods discussed in this chapter are used for the building structure as well as the insured's personal belongings, or the "contents," contained within the structure. Rates differ for these types of coverage, and insurance buyers specifically purchase each type of coverage in order to be covered for both. However, most of our discussion focuses on coverage for the structure.

[12] The Flood Insurance Reform and Modernization Act, H.R. 3121, 110th Cong. (2007) and the Flood Insurance Reform and Modernization Act, S. 2289, 110th Cong. (2007), both include provisions aimed at limiting subsidized properties.

[13] Various factors such as flood zone, structure elevation, type of structure, and amount of coverage affect the premiums.

[14] Adverse selection occurs when insurers cannot distinguish between less risky and more risky properties, although homeowners can. When premiums do not reflect differences in risk that are known to potential policyholders, those who buy insurance are often those at greatest risk for the hazards covered. Adverse selection in the market for natural catastrophe suggests that homeowners who are at the highest risk of experiencing a natural catastrophe will buy available insurance.

[15] Reinsurance is essentially insurance for insurers—that is, companies buy coverage for all or a part of a policy's liability from other insurers in order to offset exposure.

[16] This is on a conservative basis required by state insurance regulators.

[17] Two properties that are of the same NFIP risk class (for example, both are one-story, single-family homes with no basement and are elevated a certain number of feet above a reference level) are charged the same rate per $100 of insurance although they may be located in different states with differing flood experiences or rest on different topography such as a shallow floodplain versus a steep, mountainous valley.

[18] A premium system for a given insurance coverage typically takes into account expected claims costs, based on projections from relevant, credible prior experience; the administrative cost of providing the coverage, including but not limited to underwriting, sales, and claims administration; and, a margin for profits and for losses that are worse than expected. In addition, for a rate-setting system to be considered actuarially based, the premium charged to each insured should be reasonably related to the risk posed by coverage of that insured.

[19] For example, for a given property type, the rate per $100 of insurance on the first $50,000 of coverage for a single-family structure in the Regular Program (that is, what NFIP terms "basic" coverage) is $1.31. The rate per $100 of insurance on amounts in excess of $50,000 (that is, what NFIP terms "additional" coverage) is $0.10.

[20] The "1 percent annual chance flood," also known as the "100-year flood," is a statistical construct: It is a flood that has a certain discharge that produces a specific flood elevation and an estimated 1 percent chance of occurrence in any one year. In reality, the 1 percent flood represents a range of discharge and elevation values because of the uncertainties and other limitations in the information available for its computation and the resulting need to use specific types of probability distributions to portray the possibilities. The SFHA flood zones on the FIRMs can reflect varying degrees of analysis, in some cases using approximate methods while in others using more detailed methods. The accuracy of the flood hazard data depicted on the FIRMs and the delineation of the SFHA are dependent on the data limitations of the computation of the 1 percent flood and the topographic information available for the area being mapped. The variety of factors and uncertainties involved in generating flood maps render these maps less definitive and authoritative than communities frequently assume them to be—for example, many interpret the 1 percent flood line as an assurance that development above that elevation or outside that line is guaranteed to be safe from the 1 percent flood. The 1 percent flood zones reflect only existing conditions and not future development.

[21] U.S. Department of Housing and Urban Development, "Insurance and Other Programs for Financial Assistance to Flood Victims: A Report from the Secretary of the Department of Housing and Urban Development to the President, as Required by the Southeast Hurricane Disaster Relief Act of 1965," Public Law 89-339, 89th Congress, H.R. 11539, Nov. 8, 1965 (Washington, D.C.: August 1966).

[22] Property owners are underinsured when they purchase insurance coverage for less than the value of the property, either by or because of limits on the amount of available coverage. To compensate for this possibility, FEMA increases premium rates by an "underinsurance factor" that is based on claims data going back to 1978 for different zones and types of structures. More recent experience is given a greater weight in determining the factors.

[23] FEMA has taken this approach for pricing in these zones because it believes the cost of obtaining the information necessary to develop detailed flood frequency-magnitude relationships for use in the hydrologic model would be extremely high in relation to the benefits.

[24] Highly variable events (events with losses varying widely from year to year) and greatly skewed events (very rare but very large catastrophic events) such as floods, hurricanes, and earthquakes do not lend themselves to traditional actuarial pricing techniques. Results can vary dramatically from year to year and average results have little predictive value even

when gathered over a long period of time, thus rendering the use of historical flood loss experience for setting rates problematic.

[25] Studies include those by CRS, CBO, GAO, and the DHS Office of Inspector General.

[26] A FEMA official explained to us that by not updating the PELV data, NFIP essentially was assuming that the difference between the 10 percent annual chance of flood (that is, the 10-year flood) and the 1 percent annual chance of flood has not changed since the data were published in the 1970s and 1980s. FEMA told us that the PELV data have been used in such a way as to make the rates less sensitive to factors such as changes in land use, structural development, or climate trends. FEMA also noted that actuarial judgments during rate setting deal with a variety of uncertainties, such as those that go beyond simply relying on the calculation based on the hydrologic model. According to FEMA, other efforts, such as contingency loading or across-the-board rate increases on a zone, and improved floodplain management, have been made to compensate for the impact of these factors.

[27] For DELV estimates, if water reached a depth of 2 feet relative to the BFE within a one-story, no-basement structure located in the high-risk zone, 25 percent of the property's value would be damaged; however, if water reached a depth of 4 feet within the same structure, 30 percent of the property's value would be damaged.

[28] "Credible" refers to the degree of belief that the entity's prior experience is a valid predictor of future costs.

[29] American Institutes for Research, *Assessing the Adequacy of the National Flood Insurance Program's 1 Percent Flood Standard*, American Institutes for Research, prepared under subcontract to the American Institutes for Research as part of the 2001-2006 Evaluation of the National Flood Insurance Program, Water Policy Collaborative, (College Park, Md.: University of Maryland, October 2006).

[30] According to FEMA officials, zero elevation water is a depth that encompasses up to the first 5 inches of floodwater in a property. This depth is also sometimes referred to as a "carpet soaker" flood.

[31] See GAO, *Flood Map Modernization: Program Strategy Shows Promise, but Challenges Remain*, GAO-04-417 (Washington, D.C.: Mar. 31, 2004).

[32] FEMA has produced FIRMs that depict SFHAs for approximately 20,000 communities nationwide. The SFHA represents the flood that has a 1 percent annual chance of occurring in any given year, sometimes referred to as the "base flood." The base flood is the national standard used by NFIP and all federal agencies for the purposes of regulating development and requiring the purchase of flood insurance. Reliance on the 100-year flood as an adequate standard was brought into question in a recent report. See American Institutes for Research, *Assessing the Adequacy of the National Flood Insurance Program's 1 Percent Flood Standard*.

[33] FEMA has established national map quality targets under Map Modernization by tracking compliance with the Floodplain Boundary Standard and the new, validated, or updated Engineering metric. Compliance with the boundary standard indicates that the mapped floodplain matches the underlying topographic information. Compliance with the engineering metric indicates that engineering analyses used to determine the extent of the flood hazard have been either newly established or updated. The national map quality targets under Map Modernization are 75 percent of mapped stream miles compliant with boundary standard and 30 percent of mapped stream miles compliant with the engineering metric.

[34] According to FEMA, an important reason for making the grandfathering decision was that policyholders who were in compliance with their existing FIRMs should not be required to pay higher prices for new conditions of which they were previously unaware.

[35] These are pre-FIRM properties that were built before detailed flood hazard data and flood elevations were provided to the community and usually before the community enacted comprehensive regulations on floodplain regulation.

[36] FEMA officials stated that grandfathering presented a disincentive for sound floodplain management because grandfathered owners would be unaware of the true risk of flooding to their properties and would therefore be less likely to mitigate. But the officials also stated that in making this decision they took into consideration several concerns: (1) potentially higher rates that could cause property owners not to buy insurance or to lose their properties, (2) adverse reactions to FEMA as the result of these higher rates, (3) the burden on insurance agents of obtaining new map determinations and information for every policyholder, and (4) the likelihood of communities resisting new maps due to the potential for large rate increases.

[37] In most property and casualty insurance lines, state assessments are often passed through to policyholders. As a result, policyholders living in less risky locations also contribute to cover the shortfall—a scenario known as cross-subsidization. In those states where assessments cannot be passed through in some manner, private insurers must pay the assessments while at the same time paying large claims from their own policyholders. In such instances, some companies may be reluctant to continue offering coverage in the state or may become insolvent.

[38] The two types of policies in the moderate- to low-risk zones are referred to as preferred risk policies and the standard policy. The preferred risk policyholders generally pay the lowest flood rates. Preferred risk policies are available on buildings that are outside of the SFHA and have not flooded more than once.

[39] Coastal erosion is long-term erosion such that a shoreline retreats at or around an average rate over a period of decades.

[40] Shorelines rarely recede at a constant rate; instead, erosion occurs in a cyclic fashion, with seasonal and episodic influences resulting in periods of erosion, periods of stability, and periods of accretion. On shorelines suffering from long-term erosion, the periods of erosion outweigh or overwhelm the periods of stability and accretion.

[41] The H. John Heinz III Center for Science, Economics and the Environment, *Evaluation of Erosion Hazards*, Prepared for the Federal Emergency Management Agency Contract EMW-97-CO-0375, (Washington D.C.: April 2000).

[42] The National Flood Insurance Act of 1968, as amended, authorizes FEMA to carry out NFIP to enable persons to buy insurance against losses arising from flood. The statute defines flood as including sudden, flood-event-triggered collapses or subsidences of land along the shore of a body of water, but the statute's definition of flood does not include the gradual, long-term erosion that may endanger coastal communities. See 42 USC 4001, 4002 and 42 USC 4121(c).

[43] FEMA officials told us that they could likely map erosion hazard areas on FIRMs for informational, but not rate-setting, purposes under its existing authority. However, FEMA estimates the total cost of this effort could range between $50 million and $100 million.

[44] GAO, *Climate Change: Financial Risks to Federal and Private Insurers in Coming Decades Are Potentially Significant*, GAO-07-285 (Washington, D.C.: Mar. 16, 2007).

[45] This is consistent with standard actuarial practice for pricing 1-year term insurance.

[46] NFIP implemented the nationwide class-rating system because of the nature of the program and the desire to make it less complex and easier for agents and customers to understand. In the early years of the program, rates were set on a community-by-community basis. But as the number of communities participating grew, this system became unwieldy and costly to maintain. FEMA analysis indicated that from a technical perspective, this system was not essential to the estimation of flood damages since, for example, flood frequency data were found to be similar across communities.

[47] We computed the difference between the dollar amount of losses on claims paid out in that state by NFIP and the dollar amount of premiums collected in that state by NFIP.

[48] Because of the data limitations, our analysis was performed using claims and premiums data from both full-risk and explicitly subsidized policies.

[49] See appendix II for a full listing of states.

[50] Some states have a relatively large number or proportion of subsidized properties (including grandfathered properties) that generally would lead to higher expected claims relative to premiums, but we were unable to link the separate NFIP claims and premiums data at the state and zone levels in a way that would allow us to perform a more refined analysis. The limitations in setting full-risk rates that we have discussed could result in systematic mispricing relative to risk that becomes apparent only over long periods; however, our analysis included both subsidized and full risk properties, and so the results should be considered in this context.

[51] The average historical loss is calculated by adjusting the loss payouts of prior years to account for inflation and increases in the number of NFIP policies.

[52] By statute, rates may not be increased by an amount that would result in the average of such rate increases for properties within the risk classification during any 12-month period exceeding 10 percent of the average of the risk premium rates for properties within the zone.

[53] FEMA officials told us that through various calculations, they updated the $17.4 billion in losses from Katrina in 2006 to $23.2 billion presently. These calculations included an increase of 20 percent in NFIP policies and an increase of 10 percent for inflation.

[54] According to FEMA, this process was established jointly by Congress and FEMA.

[55] We found qualitatively similar results for the period 1978-2007, which includes the effects of Hurricanes Katrina, Rita, and Wilma.

CHAPTER SOURCES

The following chapters have been previously published:

Chapter 1 – This is an edited, excerpted and augmented edition of a United States Congressional Research Service publication, Report Order Code R40650, dated July 9, 2010.

Chapter 2 – This is an edited, excerpted and augmented edition of a United States Government Accountability Office publication, Report Order Code GAO-10-1063T, dated September 22, 2010.

Chapter 3 – This is an edited, excerpted and augmented edition of a United States Congressional Research Service publication, Report Order Code R41056, dated February 1, 2010.

Chapter 4 – This is an edited, excerpted and augmented edition of a United States Congressional Research Service publication, Report Order Code RL33892, dated February 6, 2009.

Chapter 5 – This is an edited, excerpted and augmented edition of a United States Government Accountability Office publication, Report Order Code GAO-09-12, dated October 2008.

INDEX

A

B

C

D

E

F

S

T

P

Q

R

L

M

N

O